D0111379

WHAT OTHERS SAY

Whether you fly once in your lifetime, once in a while, or once a week, *Life in the Skies* is an indispensable companion for you before and when you fly, even if you have no qualms at all about flying, but especially if you do. This book contains the explanations for every passenger issue I came across in my own career as an airline captain and author of my own column to answer passengers' questions. Easy to read, informative and authoritative, there is no one better to help you understand why flying remains the safest mode of travel than Captain Lim. For you white-knuckle types especially, I cannot recommend this book highly enough. 'Knowledge is power' was never more true than when trying to quell your fears, and this is *the* book to accomplish this. Happy Flying!

Captain Meryl Getline
Pilot, Author of *The World at My Feet*

Captain Lim has done the world of flying a great service with the publication of his website and now his book. He clearly answers all those questions and more those who enjoy flying have always wanted to ask. But he has performed a special service for those people I work with – fearful flyers – who dearly wish they could enjoy the benefits of commercial aviation if only they better manage their thoughts, feelings and behaviours. Almost all fearful flyers would do well to understand how commercial aviation operates, from its basic safety operations, through to aircraft design and crew training, as well as air traffic control: all those things that come to together to make flying the safe form of public transport it is – only escalators and elevators are safer on a person carried per mile basis. Over the years, Captain Lim and I have met in person and maintained a knowledge exchange we believe is useful for our respective audiences. For me it's the 1 in 6 to 1 in 12 of the general population who expresses a significant fear of flying. I heartily recommend Captain Lim's book for that population as well as anyone, trainee pilots included, with an interest in commercial aviation from someone with impeccable credentials.

Les Posen
Clinical Psychologist, Fellow, Australian Psychological Society

"Whether you are a frequent flyer, fearful flyer, an aspiring student pilot or just inquisitive about the intricacies of aviation – this book is for you. *Life in the Skies* depicts just how flying is the safest mode of travel by covering a gamut of topics and by answering unique passenger questions. You're going to learn a lot from Captain Lim's straightforward and accurate writing!"

Captain Doug Morris

Captain, Author of *From the Flight Deck*

It is no exaggeration to say that Captain Lim can almost be compared to the walking Google on the subject of aviation. His new book, *Life in the Skies* is comprehensive, well-written and thoroughly-researched to disseminate information on the safety aspects of flying. If you are someone who has aviophobia or just a pilot wannabe, I assure you that *Life in the Skies* is a must-read!"

Yvonne Lee

Ex-stewardess, Author of *The Sky is Crazy* and *Madness Aboard*

Captain Lim is that rarest of aviators – an authority who can take one of the most misunderstood and widely feared realms that exists – commercial flying – and makes it comprehensible and captivating to the lay readers. Every pilot wishes that his passengers better understood the realities of flight but few have the dedication and talent of Captain Lim who actually makes it happen.

Patrick Smith

Pilot, Author of *Ask the Pilot* and *Cockpit Confidential*,
Host of www.askthepilot.com

How safe is safe? Short and simple, yet one of the most profound among the many questions fearful flyers have asked of aviation safety experts, for many years. Captain Lim's book, *Life in the Skies*, answers that question in a manner which is both comprehensive and captivating. He combines interesting facts of aviation history, with recent developments in pilot training, hardware/software technology, and even new and better air traffic control procedures – clearly explaining how it all works towards improving airline safety stats to levels never before thought possible.

We operated a 'Fearful Flyers Forum', as part of our Airline Safety Website, for several years. I believe I have heard just about every question possible that has been asked by those who came to us for help and understanding. It is evident, both from his website and now this book that Captain Lim has heard and responded to all those same questions, many times over. He is the ultimate authority on virtually any airline safety issue that one can think of, in my opinion. *Life in the Skies* is a valuable manual for any passenger who understands that the more he knows about how airliners function and how highly-trained pilots ensure each flight is operated with *safety* as the number one goal, the more his anxiety will be reduced to almost nothing of consequence. Knowledge *is* power, and that is what each reader will gain from Captain Lim's very interesting book.

Robert J. Boser
Editor-in-Chief, AirlineSafety.com

It has been a privilege to have had Captain Lim fly for AirAsia X and share his in-depth expertise as one of our Training & Standards instructors. With safety and reliability at the centre of our operating model, we have invested in brand new aircraft with latest technology and equip our pilots with rigorous training programs. However, I personally feel that the best thing we can do to promulgate strong safety practices is to have an open culture where our crew can share their experiences and speak up without fear or favour. Captain Lim's enthusiasm in sharing his knowledge reflects this spirit.

Azran Osman-Rani
Chief Executive Officer, AirAsia X Berhad

Can a computer geek who plays flight simulation games help to land a commercial airplane in an emergency? Believe it or not, Captain Lim's book actually answers that question. This should give you an indication of the tone of this tome. Yes, air travel safety is serious business, but Captain Lim, with his years of experience and knowledge, provides assurances through fascinating, humorous, sometimes surprising facts, fancies and anecdotes. I've always wondered whether turbulence is dangerous and what really happens if you switch on your mobile phone on a plane. This book answers it all.

Allan Koay
Journalist, *The Star*

Although the statistics will tell you that air travel is one of the safest forms of transportation, what really comforts a traveller is not numbers on a page but relevant and accessible anecdotal explanations to any conceivable topic surrounding the flying experience. At AirAsia we declare "Now Everyone Can Fly" but after Captain Lim's *Life in the Skies*, now there are no more excuses for anyone not to fly!

Bo Lingam

Chief Operating Officer, AirAsia Group

If you're someone who equates air travel to getting socked multiple times in the head – scary, painful and potentially life-threatening – Captain Lim is your liberator. *Life in the Skies* is the culmination of decades spent in the industry, reading, researching and flying, by him. It is a fascinating, well-researched manual backed with compelling case studies about everything you want to know before you board, or fly, that plane. Honest and genuine, Captain Lim is an industry veteran who doesn't try to whitewash the inherent dangers in flying, however minimal, but explains thoroughly the safety mechanisms that can be employed in such scenarios. Do yourself a favour and read it. Don't let the fear of flying stop you from crossing things off your bucket list!

Louisa Lim

Journalist, *The Star*

From dispelling common myths about air travel to sharing anecdotes that appeal to the general public and not merely aviation enthusiasts, Captain Lim is clear proof of wisdom that comes with age and experience. The stories in this book are not just eye-opening; they are reassuring as well, informing readers on air travel issues and how safe it is to fly today.

Aireen Omar

Chief Executive Officer, AirAsia Berhad

LIFE IN THE SKIES

EVERYTHING YOU WANT TO KNOW ABOUT FLYING

CAPTAIN LIM KHOY HING

© 2013 Lim Khoy Hing
Photographs by AirAsia Group and Lim Khoy Hing

Published by Marshall Cavendish Editions
An imprint of Marshall Cavendish International (Asia) Pte Ltd
1 New Industrial Road, Singapore 536196

Reprinted in 2014

Other Marshall Cavendish Offices:
Marshall Cavendish Corporation. 99 White Plains Road, Tarrytown NY 10591-9001, USA
• Marshall Cavendish International (Thailand) Co Ltd. 253 Asoke, 12th Flr, Sukhumvit 21
Road, Klongtoey Nua, Wattana, Bangkok 10110, Thailand • Marshall Cavendish (Malaysia)
Sdn Bhd, Times Subang, Lot 46, Subang Hi-Tech Industrial Park, Batu Tiga, 40000 Shah
Alam, Selangor Darul Ehsan, Malaysia

Marshall Cavendish is a trademark of Times Publishing Limited

National Library Board Singapore Cataloguing in Publication Data
Lim, Khoy Hing.
Life in the skies : everything you want to know about flying / Captain Lim Khoy Hing. –
Singapore : Marshall Cavendish Editions, 2013.
pages cm
ISBN : 978-981-4484-13-8 (paperback)

1. Flight. 2. Aeronautics. 3. Aerodynamics.

TL575
629.1325 -- dc23   OCN 855041795

Printed by Vivar Printing Sdn. Bhd, Lot 25, Rawang Integrated Industrial Park,
Jalan Batu Arang, 48000 Rawang, Selangor Darul Ehsan, Malaysia.

DEDICATION

This book is dedicated to my wife, Koh Hui Ching;
my daughter and son-in-law, Lim Pei Mun and Jeff Shotton;
my son and daughter-in-law, Lim Kok Chian and Vivian Chok;
and my grandchildren,
Alex, Marcus, Annabelle, Yi Yin and Hao Vern.

CONTENTS

PART III
Coming down to earth: When it's time to land

PART IV
Interlude: Human affairs

PART V
A bit on the airline business and their flying machines

PART VI
Welcome to the future

FOREWORD

Flying. For most, the idea conjures up images of exotic locales, the prospect of new experiences, the promise of adventure. For others, it recalls the more prosaic monotony of security checks and waiting in airport lounges. But either way, it remains a wonderful way to travel that bridges continents and connects lives in a matter of hours.

However, there's another side to flying seldom seen by the public and less often written about – life inside the cockpit. The men and women tasked with getting us to our destinations in safe and timely fashion are easily some of the world's most highly trained and heavily tested individuals, yet little is known about them.

This book aims to address that shortcoming. Writing in a clear, lucid voice, Captain Lim sheds light on what it means to be a pilot, drawing on his more than 40 years of flying.

Chock-full of insights and entertaining anecdotes, this volume is indispensable to anyone who has ever wondered what goes on behind the scenes before, during and after each flight.

From his days training for the Royal Malaysian Air Force in England to his adventures with Malaysia Airlines and AirAsia, Captain Lim demonstrates an unmistakable passion for flying that only those who dedicate their lives to piloting can.

Along the way, he also tackles frequently asked questions: Is flying really safer than driving? Why must cabin lights dimmed before take off and landing? Can an aircraft fly upside-down? How do you land a plane when all engines are out? Why can't electronic devices be used during certain stages of flying? What happens when lightning strikes an aircraft?

This book takes on all that and more, with a strong emphasis on safety. Some of the answers may surprise, some may not, but all help explain the sometimes difficult decisions pilots have to make, even if they prove unpopular.

Above all, it is a testament to the competence of and care provided by the special breed of people who ply the friendly skies and make it possible for everyone to fly. It's my honour and pleasure to call Captain Lim a colleague, and I'm sure this book will make a welcome addition to the catalogue.

TONY FERNANDES
Group Chief Executive Officer, AirAsia
September 2013

ACKNOWLEDGEMENTS

The catalyst for this book was Carlos, from Brazil; he and a few others who were loyal readers of askcaptainlim.com, who wanted to know when I might compile all my answers about flying into a book. They provided the questions for this book, which they posed to me on askcaptainlim.com, and I would like to sincerely thank them for the kind interest and warm encouragement they have shown.

It's taken a long time for this book to become reality. This is partly due to my belief that my writing style is quintessentially Malaysian and bears a very Asian outlook. I also felt it lacked the fluency of seasoned writers, something which may not be welcomed by an international audience. So to improve my writing skills, I started to write and contribute free articles to AirAsia's inflight magazine, *Travel 3Sixty*, and that was how I got started writing seriously.

I would like to thank Tan Sri Tony Fernandes for taking time out of his incredibly hectic schedule to pen the foreword, and for kindly agreeing to sponsor this book.

Many thanks to the first managing editor of *Travel 3Sixty*, Ng Li Fern, and her successor, R. Rajendra, whose expert editing and skilful input lent a professional touch to my articles, and internal editor Yow Hong Chieh for fine-tuning this book. I'd also like to mention Chua Sook Mun, Dato' Kamarudin Meranun, Kathleen Tan, Christine Chong, Jason Tan, Glenn Wray, Mindy Pang, Adzhar bin Ibrahim, Al-Ishsal Ishak, Vikram Noronha, Ooi Mei Ying, Nianci Phang, Lau Mun Lay, Nadiah Tan, Angelina Corrina Fernandez, Rengeeta Kaur Rendava, Beverly Rodrigues, Kan Seak Hong, Adam Lee, Fazlina Bee, Matthew Mok, Yvonne Lady Diana and Hazel Teh, for helping to make this book a success. I am also very grateful to many others who have, in one way or another, been involved in this endeavour.

I would also like to thank Captain Meryl Getline, one of the few first Boeing 777 lady captains and author of *The World at My Feet*, who scrutinised my draft; United Airlines Captain Robert J. Boser, editor of airlinesafety.com; Patrick Smith of *Ask The Pilot* fame; Doug Morris, Canadian Airlines A320 Captain; Australian clinical psychologist Les Posen, who shared his knowledge on how air travellers can conquer their fear of flying; Yvonne Lee, an ex-colleague and author of *The Sky is Crazy* and *Madness Aboard*; Louisa Lim and Allan Koay, journalists from *The Star* newspaper; Azran Rani-Omar, CEO of AirAsia X Bhd; Aireen Omar, CEO of AirAsia Bhd and Bo Lingam, COO of AirAsia Group; for their generous comments and reviews.

My deepest gratitude is to my daughter, Lim Pei Mun who reads and ensures my articles are easily understood despite the colloquial Malaysian English used. She also keeps me in check when I get too technical in my explanations. And to my son, Lim Kok Chian, who has been instrumental in updating my old, static website to something more dynamic.

Finally, my deepest thanks goes to my wonderful wife, Koh Hui Ching, who has been eternally patient with me for spending so much of my time working on my computer and the book, especially after work!

PART I

THINGS YOU'VE ALWAYS WANTED
TO KNOW ABOUT PILOTS BEFORE
STEPPING ON A PLANE

CHAPTER 1

THIS IS HOW WE DO IT
Introducing safe flying

How much does an average person know about air travel? Most people get their impression of flying and of pilots from Hollywood movies. One popular show was *Flight*, starring Academy Award winner Denzel Washington, which became a critically acclaimed box-office blockbuster. Quite a few readers wrote in with questions about the film, so I was compelled to watch it.

Flight turned out to be a highly entertaining action flick about a pilot who crash-lands his plane with 102 passengers on board. He saves the majority of them and is hailed as a hero, but all is not well as he comes under the scrutiny of the National Transportation Safety Board when tests reveal heavy usage of alcohol and drugs.

The movie opens with a scene of the captain with a rather naked flight attendant. Scenes like this reinforce public perception that the crew are often promiscuous. Readers frequently ask if it's possible for airline pilots to have successful marriages despite travelling to exotic destinations with good-looking cabin crew.

Pilots are human beings, just like anyone else. Some are loyal and others are unfaithful. Some have excellent and lasting marriages while others have less successful ones. Admittedly, there are more opportunities to stray in this profession and there's no need to lie about working late or explain the whiff of women's perfume on the uniform. After all, flying around the world with pretty flight attendants is all part of the job.

Wives of pilots have asked me about signs of infidelity. Far from being a marriage counsellor, I can only relay general observations about such issues in the aviation industry. A straying spouse may become more vain or play hide-and-seek with his partner. An unfaithful husband may suddenly turn into a big spender or a master at arranging his schedule. Sometimes, he may seem edgy on the phone or inefficient in bed.

But I'm no relationship expert so please do not take my words as gospel. If you suspect something amiss, it would be advisable to seek a marriage counsellor and not use the points here to confirm infidelity.

WHAT THE MOVIE IS *REALLY* ABOUT

But I would like to think that *Flight* is really a movie about air safety, and it gives me an opportunity to present my views about it and the reality of a pilot's life. Take, for instance, alcohol consumption by airline pilots – the movie's depiction of an alcoholic captain sniffing oxygen in a cockpit prior to his flight may lead some to wonder if this actually happens. In reality, pilots have strict rules that they must abide by. Oxygen inhalation inside the cockpit to clear a hangover is not a standard practice.

STRANGERS WORKING TOGETHER

Due to the scheduling system that rosters flight crew for the scores of flights the airline operates throughout the world, it's impossible for one pilot to know another very well. There are times where the two have never even met prior to the actual flight. How then can they hope to cooperate and cope well, especially in emergencies? It comes down to flight trainers, who ensure that strict standard operating procedures are adhered to at all times. Even standard phrases for challenges and responses made by the captain and co-pilot to each other are used to avoid confusion.

After the captain, we often hear the term 'co-pilot' but the more appropriate salutation would be 'first officer', as this individual is second-in-command should the captain be incapacitated. The first officer is therefore trained to handle the aircraft safely in any eventuality, especially when the pilot in command is in no condition to fly safely.

To begin with, the pre-flight briefing reminds pilots to review threats and error management so that their flight will progress safely. These days, a first officer is trained to make a report directly or anonymously if he or she feels the captain has compromised the safety of the flight. The smelling of alcohol would definitely be a red flag. So, a chronic drinker like the captain in *Flight* wouldn't last long in his career. Even if there are a few co-pilots who decide not to report him, there'll be others who will.

RESPECT THE WEATHER

In the movie, the captain takes off in heavy rain. This is not normal practice. A cautious captain would wait for the rain to stop or at least turn into a light drizzle. This is because there are many hazards that come with torrential rain, such as reduced visibility or increased risk of running off the runway in the event of an aborted take-off.

Similarly, in an attempt to avoid severe turbulence in a thunderstorm, the captain in the movie increases speed to the maximum limit. While this probably adds drama to the story, it is contrary to real world operating procedures where a pilot would actually reduce speed, just like how you would slow down if you had to drive over a pothole. Planes are not structurally designed to fly at high-speed in turbulence.

THE CAPTAIN IS A BAD-ASS HERO WHO CAN FLY UPSIDE DOWN. NOT.

There's more added drama that you don't get in real-life which is shown in the movie: The captain is arrogant and condescending and the first officer is meek, being frightened and clueless at times. This is not how an actual pilot would behave and only reinforces the myth that the co-pilot is an apprentice who merely assists the captain. A real co-pilot is a well-trained first officer who is assertive and competent.

Even though stoned out of his mind, the captain in *Flight* skilfully manoeuvres his plane in an uncontrolled dive and resorts to an unorthodox flight procedure – inverting the plane – to save the day. This led one reader to ask if a commercial airliner can actually fly upside down. Yes, it is possible to fly inverted momentarily on certain planes but not on a modern airliner as there are mechanisms that protect it against such a manoeuvre during normal flights.

On the Airbus, it is not possible to bank beyond 67 degrees left or right, so it is impossible to turn the plane upside down. However, when a plane is not in the 'normal law' – usually after some technical failure – this bank protection is lost. Only then is it possible to invert a commercial plane temporarily. To date, no pilot has ever done so intentionally during an actual commercial flight, only in simulator training and once, during a demonstration flight, on a Boeing 707.

The heroic protagonist in the movie saves a diving plane by turning it upside down, before rolling it the right-side up again, in time for a fairly successful crash landing in a field.

Even the most experienced and competent (not to mention sober) pilot might find such a manoeuvre next to impossible to pull off safely. But real life just isn't interesting enough for a Hollywood movie.

While *Flight* is a rivetting and suspenseful piece of entertainment, if these flying myths aren't dispelled, even the most hardened of air travellers may start to worry about the flight crew, their competency and state of mind.

FLYER, KNOW THY AIRLINE

Fear of flying, or pteromerhanophobia, is a real and debilitating anxiety for many passengers, mostly exacerbated by lack of information. Not being in control is bad enough but ignorance and the refusal to seek knowledge can lead to irrational fear that will forever haunt the passenger.

Speaking of the lack of information, a fellow pilot-blogger was surprised at the responses he received on one post. After he'd written favourably about the safety record of the low-cost carrier I flew with, his post drew worried queries from some travellers, wondering whether there was a loosening of safety systems on low cost carriers, since their tickets were cheaper than the norm.

Many travellers think that low-cost flights are inherently less safe than full-service flights. This is a common misconception and a perception that is rather difficult for any low-cost carrier to shake off, but it makes them even more vigilant about maintaining their safety record. In reality, a good airline's fares can be affordable because it does away with the costly frills of air travel, not because it compromises on safety.

How safe is an airline, any airline? That's an easy one. Check out how the airline trains its pilots. A safe airline is one that spares no cost and puts in maximum effort to train its pilots to fly you to your destination safely.

AirAsia, voted the 'World's Best Low-Cost Airline' five times in a row (2009 to 2013) by Skytrax, has six flight simulators at its disposal to help train top quality pilots. This contributes to its safety record.

Are you one of those who worries that your plane may collide with another in mid-air? This once happened to Saudi Arabia and Kazakhstan Airlines in 1996 while flying over India. It claimed 349 lives. But these days, rest assured that all Airbus A320/330/340s are equipped with the Traffic and Collision Avoidance System, which was not installed on the planes involved in the 1996 accident.

It's not all left in the hands of computers. Pilots are regularly tested to ensure they know how to avoid colliding with another aircraft mid-air. How? By simulating difficult scenarios to test the pilot's skills, such as having more than one aircraft heading towards your own. If only car drivers could practise for these kinds of scenarios.

AirAsia, one of the largest operators of A320s in the world, also has one of the more stringent maintenance procedures in the industry. For its efforts, the airline won a coveted operational excellence award from Airbus for 'Exceptional Technical Performance' in 2009.

One of the six flight simulators at the AirAsia Academy.

AirAsia is a low-cost airline with a good safety record, one that has lasted since its launch in 2001. This was achieved through the following.

USING SAFETY PROGRAMMES

Pilot-training is just the start; there are also essential programmes and tools that airlines employ to enhance safety. One such tool is the **Flight Operational Quality Assurance** (FOQA), which is probably the most important safety tool used by quality airlines to monitor how safely their pilots are flying. It provides essential information such as how fast, how slow, how high and how low the plane is flying – akin to having a safety inspector watch over the pilot's shoulder. FOQA is costly to adopt but airlines that care about safety will use it regardless of the expense.

Another safety tool adopted by AirAsia to ensure safe airline operations is **Crew Resources Management** (CRM), an essential training programme that focuses on the human factors in aviation. Why is CRM essential? Although pilots can be professionally and technically competent, they're only human, and there are some with less than satisfactory people skills. Take, for instance, the captain's word; in the past, this was final and whatever the captain ordered was to be followed. So the supporting crew sometimes felt too intimidated to speak up even if they disagreed. This lack of effective communication were the cause of some major airline accidents, so today, the programme trains younger pilots to be assertive and speak up if they disagree with the captain's decision.

In short, CRM training (among others) improves communication among the crew; it coaches the captain to delegate his or her authority to lighten workload in an emergency, ensuring the safe and proper monitoring during flight of the automated equipment at all times.

HIGH-RISK BEHAVIOUR

Compared with other modes of travel, flying is one of the safest means of getting from one place to another, as well as the fastest. More than three million people fly around the world every day without issues. As far back as the year 2000, more than one billion people flew throughout the world and there were only 20 fatal air accidents in that year.

In the US alone, fewer people have died in commercial plane accidents over the last 60 years than were killed in car crashes over an average three-month period. About 115 people die every day in automobile accidents – that's about one death every 13 minutes! The statistics for road fatalities in Malaysia are equally worrying – a director-general of the Malaysian Road Safety Department reported that an average of 17 people are killed daily on Malaysian roads. That's 6,205 people a year in a country with a population of about 29 million.

So, how safe is 'safe'? 'Safe' is a very relative term. Maybe I can explain it like this: The safest airline in the world is one without any planes or has planes that never fly. But don't take my word for it, listen to the experts:

> The risks that scare people and the risks that kill people are very different. When hazard is high and outrage is low (car accidents), people under-react. And when hazard is low and outrage is high (air crashes), they overreact.
>
> —**Peter Sandman,** *Risk Communications Consultant*

> If you are looking for perfect safety, you will do well to sit on a fence and watch the birds!
>
> —**Wilbur Wright,** *inventor of the world's first successful plane in 1903*

Still, only one in 16 passengers is really comfortable travelling by plane and one in six would avoid flying if they could help it. But their fear of flying is probably based on a lack of knowledge. If they knew the efforts the airline industry puts into creating a safe and comfortable flying experience, they might enjoy their flights better. I'll let you in on a few interesting facts about the pilots and crew who, among others, are tasked with transporting you safely to your destination.

WHAT DO PILOTS EAT?

The food that your captain or first officers eat before they prepare for a flight or when in the air are different from that for passengers. Some seafood, such as oysters, crab meat and squid, are not generally served to them as they could potentially cause food poisoning if not well-prepared. Also, the captain and first officer do not eat the same food in case both get stomach cramps simultaneously, jeopardising the safety of a flight.

WHAT MUST THE PILOT SEE?

Pilots have to maintain a high standard of health and are required to visit the doctor for a medical check-up every six months if they're over 40 years old.

When I was young, I was told a pilot must have 20/20 vision without glasses. That was probably true for fighter pilots who required perfect vision in order to engage enemy aircraft in dogfights. The reality is, airline pilots can wear glasses. In fact, I do so when I fly.

Pilots today don't need to have perfect vision if the deficiency can be corrected by lenses. What's most important for pilots is to be able to read flight instruments and see images clearly, as objects tracked by radar are shown on the instrument panel in front of them. For example, aircraft on a collision course are captured on the instrument screens and pilots are instantly warned to take evasive action.

WHAT HAPPENS WHEN SOMETHING HAPPENS TO THE CAPTAIN?

Pilots are generally a healthy lot. However, there have been the odd occasions where pilots have suffered heart attacks during a flight. This is extremely rare but first officers are trained to take over in such emergencies.

There are special procedures for them to detect any subtle incapacitation of the captain while flying. First officers are drilled to look for correct verbal responses from the captain during the critical phases of flight, especially when performing auto-landing in marginal weather.

For instance, at 1,000 feet above ground level, the captain must respond to the first officer's two challenges (reminders), such as the '1,000 feet!' call.

Less than 500 feet above ground level, when a response such as 'Check!' is required, the captain is only given one reminder to read back. If he fails to do so, the first officer must assume control immediately. It would be too late to find out why he wasn't reacting otherwise.

WHAT IF A PASSENGER GETS A HEART ATTACK IN MID-AIR?

A concerned guest once wrote to ask about the kind of training the crew receives to provide medical assistance should a passenger become sick or suffer a heart attack in mid-air.

All cabin crew are trained in First Aid and Cardiopulmonary Resuscitation (CPR). They are taught basic cardiac life support and the use of defibrillators on board the plane. They undergo courses that cover all aspects of First Aid, as well as occupational health, altitude physiology and details of medical equipment carried on board. In addition, they must attend annual refresher courses on these and on CPR practices.

Even so, the flight crew is trained in basic First Aid and the use of life-support equipment only. This means that they will rely on professionals for more serious medical emergencies. Hence the announcement, 'Is there a doctor on board?' is often heard whenever a more serious emergency arises.

In the United Kingdom, there is no legal duty for a doctor to offer assistance in an emergency although the General Medical Council considers that such a duty exists. The question of legal liability for medical emergencies on board aircraft is confusing because the law varies from country to country. Several major airlines have now taken out insurance policies indemnifying doctors who come forward to help.

HOW WILL A PASSENGER GET TO THE HOSPITAL IF THE PLANE IS IN MID-AIR?

Aircraft commanders have the discretion to make a diversion during medical emergencies based on the severity of the passenger's condition. Of course, they will consult with all parties – doctors in the plane or on the ground, and the airlines, before coming to a decision.

Sometimes the affected guest may be too ill or unconscious, and therefore cannot be consulted. If the commander's decision is to divert, he does so because a life is at stake. On one AirAsia X flight on an Airbus A330 from Kuala Lumpur to Melbourne, the captain had to make an emergency diversion to Alice Springs for immediate medical attention when one of the guests became very sick.

WHAT DOES 'FROM BOTTLE TO THROTTLE' MEAN?

And here we come back to the premise of *Flight* – the drink-flying hero captain. So how does the airline industry handle cases of pilots who drink a little too much? Who stops a pilot and gives him a breathalyser test if he is found to have gone too far partying throughout the night prior to his flight?

In Malaysia, so far, there hasn't been any case of a drunken pilot being charged with flying with blood alcohol content beyond the prescribed limit of 0.04 per cent for flying (versus 0.08 per cent for driving). However, there are many practices in place to ensure the person who pilots your flight is fully sober and in control of his or her mental and physical faculties.

Pilot alcohol-consumption is strictly regulated in the airline industry. The general rule is that pilots must not drink at least eight hours before assuming the role of a crew member, as they might still be under the influence of alcohol. Hence the saying 'eight hours bottle to throttle'. Some airlines have slightly different policies. For AirAsia, it is '10 hours bottle to throttle', meaning there is to be no alcohol consumption 10 hours prior to a flight.

Interestingly, jetliners no longer use throttles, as was the case with propeller planes. They now use thrust-levers to propel the planes to greater speed. But the use of this aviator term 'bottle to throttle' has stuck because it rhymes so well.

There can be serious penalties for breaking the rule. In one case in the US, two airline pilots who had been drinking prior to their flight were sentenced to between two-and-a-half and five years in jail. Also, airlines will suspend or fire pilots for any serious charge, conviction or even on the suspicion of drunken flying.

In another incident, a Boeing 777 airline pilot at London Heathrow was arrested minutes before take-off on suspicion of being drunk. It was a tip-off from a member of the ground staff who suspected the captain had been boozing before the flight. In countries like the US, the Transportation Security Agency conducts random alcohol checks on crew members. In other cases, airport security officials who suspect that a pilot has been drinking during his body search can tip off the authorities.

Flying is a very demanding and unforgiving undertaking. Anything that impairs the pilot's ability to work efficiently in the cockpit is an invitation to disaster.

CHAPTER 2

SPEAKING UP SAVES LIVES

Good men and women are trained to say no to the boss

There's no room in the cockpit for 'yes-men' among pilots. When lives are at stake, co-pilots are trained to speak up and even wrest control to land the aircraft safely.

The old belief among co-pilots was that the captain could do no wrong. First officers had no choice but to adhere to the chain of command. But what if the captain makes a serious mistake? Can his error be allowed in the face of dire consequences?

From some air accidents in the past, it would appear that certain co-pilots faced difficulties in challenging their captains. This reluctance to question authority might have been brought forward from the past, when senior captains were ex-military pilots and their commands were not to be questioned. There is also an East Asian culture of deference to the wisdom of an older person. The captain was 'God', someone not to be argued with even if the wrong decision was made.

In terms of civil aviation, this is no longer valid where safety is concerned. More than 75 per cent of air crashes involve human error, which can be attributed to failures of leadership, team coordination and decision-making. Constant and rigorous training in Crew Resources Management (CRM) and Evidential Base Training (EBT) for air crew are among some of the steps that have been put in place to mitigate against these possibilities. (More on these in the next chapter.)

SAY WHAT YOU MEAN, AND MEAN WHAT YOU SAY

In 1977, two Boeing 747 charter flights from the now-defunct Pan American World Airways and KLM collided at Tenerife in the Canary Islands. It was the worst air accident of the century, claiming nearly 600 lives.

The captain of the said KLM flight who took off without clearance was also the chief pilot in charge of training, a man of prestige, respect and trust. The co-pilot who was on duty with him did not dare question the captain and assumed his superior was always right. In fact, this co-pilot had been trained by the same senior instructor a few months earlier. The co-pilot found himself in a tough position, but if he had questioned the captain, both may still be alive today, along with 600 others.

In January 2004, a Boeing 737-300 went into the Red Sea shortly after takeoff from Sharm el-Sheikh International Airport. The captain was not just one of Egypt's most experienced pilots, he was a highly decorated war hero in the Egyptian Air Force.

During the flight, the captain suffered spatial disorientation (a loss in the sense of direction and position in flight) and made a mistake in the turn. The co-pilot was well aware of the error but was unwilling to challenge his more experienced superior. This deference and inability to speak up at that crucial juncture resulted in an accident that could have been averted.

These are just a few examples of many instances when lower ranking officers chose to remain silent out of fear and misplaced respect, knowing fully well their superiors had made fatal decisions. The inability to assert good judgment and show disapproval in the presence of a superior led to these fatal human errors.

FOCUS ON THE IMPORTANT THINGS

In a TriStar accident in 1972, the lack of crew coordination, communication and delegation of duties were evident. Here, three highly qualified flight crew members comprising the captain, first officer and flight engineer were so engrossed in solving a minor problem on board that no one was actually flying the plane. All of them became so fixated on the landing gear light that no one noticed that the autopilot had been disengaged by accident.

An example of good crew coordination and teamwork was evident in the incident involving a DC-10 in Sioux City, Iowa, in 1989. The plane suffered a catastrophic failure of its tail-mounted engine that led to loss of all flight controls. While the cause of the accident was not due to pilot error, on checking the maintenance history, it was determined that a mechanic had not done his job properly and certain important inspections had not been carried out. Even though the accident was classified as mechanical failure, the root cause can still be traced back to human error. The crew, which had been trained in CRM were able to handle a very difficult situation – as a team – and bring the aircraft safely back to ground, saving the lives of at least 185 people.

Another success story is that of the Qantas Airbus A380 flight from Singapore to Sydney. The plane suffered an exploding engine failure that also caused numerous other problems to the structure. Mercifully, quick action and coordinated effort from crew members in the cockpit saved all 469 lives onboard. They, too, were well-trained in CRM.

Before CRM training became mandatory for all airlines, pilots and crew used to work autonomously. The gist of CRM is the emphasis on teamwork, coordination and delegation of duties. These were non-existent in the past, when the captain was considered the authority and his word was law.

In the TriStar case mentioned above, the captain did not delegate responsibility to any of his crew at all. Someone must always be flying the aircraft. By not delegating and getting too preoccupied with the problem at hand, the captain and his team breached the first golden rule of the Airbus flying philosophy – Fly, Navigate and Communicate.

MANAGING YOUR BOSS

The importance of CRM is emphasised in all the half-yearly pilot checks. Evidential Base Training, such as recreating scenarios of recent catastrophic events, is included in the flight check syllabus to assess the reactions of the co-pilot. These scenarios not only demand that the team coordinate and work together, they also check if team members know when to speak up and to be assertive.

For example, during one section of the Pilot Check flight, the captain is told to act in an overpowering and rigid manner, overly fixating on continuing with the flight, regardless of the safety of the plane and its passengers. During the course of the training, when the captain intentionally makes wrong decisions, the training module will test how co-pilots react and take control by defying their superior.

It is implicitly drummed into the trainees' heads that it is perfectly fine to stand up, speak up and wrest control from their bosses when precious lives are at stake. However, the co-pilot is trained to take over by employing set procedures and appropriate phrases that are urgent but non-confrontational. The airline industry also recognises the predicament of a subordinate crew member and gives him protection against insubordination should such an event occur.

While I was flying, I always encouraged my first officers to speak up if they had any questions or to query anything they were uncomfortable with. Pride and ego have no place in the cockpit and this is indoctrinated into the flight crew constantly. You can be sure that the team flying passengers to their destination have also been subjected to the same messages time and time again. The safety of all passengers is always of the utmost importance.

Flying is so much safer than it used to be. The airline industry has put in a lot of effort to reduce human error and trainers play a very important role to ensure pilots are reminded of the pitfalls of poor CRM. Young pilots are encouraged to be assertive and say no to their bosses at appropriate times.

CHAPTER 3

THE THINGS WE DO FOR FLYING

Because you can't pop open the hood in mid-air

If you drive, do you check if there's sufficient engine oil before you shoot off to wherever you're going? Not many drivers do so. However, if you neglect to check and your car engine overheats and catches fire, you can easily jump out of the car and make a hasty exit. This luxury is not possible while flying.

So it is critical to check a plane's engine oil before each flight. It's just one of the many items in a detailed checklist that must be scrutinised before every flight. The pilot can't get out of the cockpit to check on the engines while a plane is in mid-air!

Meticulous pre-flight inspection is part of a pilot's job, and just a tiny part of a pilot's role in ensuring that passengers are transported to their destination without drama. And if something unexpected happens anyway, pilots are trained to rapidly recognise and manage emergencies safely. Here are some of the ways.

STAYING SHARP

All pilots in the airline industry are required to go through 'base checks', or Check Rides, at least once every six months. This includes demonstrating their handling skills and procedural and system knowledge. Such Check Rides are usually programmed to run for two to three days in a flight simulator.

Each Check Ride consists of four hours of exercises on stress and anxiety management, and emergencies that could occur. These range from engine failure and fires, to flight control problems and loss of electrical power, among others. In a three-year cycle, a pilot would have undergone testing for all the major failures.

Imagine practising handling the plane during engine or brake failure and other kinds of emergencies over and over again until you can do so safely – that is what pilots are tested on almost every six months. Pilots train so extensively on these simulators that those who experience actual inflight emergencies generally report that they didn't panic. The simulator had prepared them well for real-life situations.

Pilots also have a well-developed ability to multi-task, such as listening to all air traffic control instructions while monitoring cockpit instruments during flight. Additionally, they are very vigilant and always ready to react should a warning from the plane's computer appear. In case you're still wondering whether they really can handle the heat, here are some situations a pilot is always ready for.

STUFF A PILOT MUST KEEP IN MIND. ALWAYS.

A pilot is one of the most checked and tested individuals on earth. This individual needs to be on top of the game from the day they earn their wings right up to retirement. After all, a pilot is entrusted with a hugely expensive machine and its even more priceless contents – the passengers. The mandatory half-yearly base check for pilots covers potential flight emergencies. It ensures all pilots are physically, mentally and emotionally capable of handling an aircraft and safeguarding the welfare of their passengers.

The pilot's many mandatory skills, apart from being able to fly adeptly, can be found in the 'magic bag' known as the pilot's brain. It contains 10 of the most critical things to keep in mind, or 'memory items', the drills that help a pilot recognise, and react to, emergencies.

A pilot memorises many checklists but need not memorise each and every potential emergency that can happen in mid-air. However, there are critical events that require split-second solutions and decisions to avert disaster. Hence, the mandatory '10 Memory Items' devised by Airbus to cope with emergency situations are as follows.

MEMORY ITEM NUMBERS 1 AND 2: THE WIND IS COMING FROM UP, DOWN, OR ALL AROUND – HOW TO HANDLE WIND SHEAR BEFORE TAKE-OFF AND DURING FLIGHT

Wind shear is a sudden change of wind velocity and/or direction, vertically or horizontally. In August 1985, a Delta Air Lines TriStar in the US crashed while landing at Dallas-Fort Worth International Airport due to wind shear that the pilot could not address in time. This situation can be avoided today because the aircraft is installed with a system that predicts wind shear and, warns the pilot to either abort the take-off (Memory Item Number 1) or, if the aircraft is caught whilst taking off, to apply maximum thrust immediately (Memory Item Number 2).

MEMORY ITEM NUMBER 3: HOW CLOSE ARE WE TO THE GROUND AGAIN?

It depends. The ground, or 'terrain', is a relative term. To pilots, mountains or skyscrapers are 'terrain' too. Pilots now have an Enhanced Ground Proximity Warning System

(EGPWS) that alerts them when the aircraft is dangerously close to a mountain. The EGPWS uses the aircraft's position, altitude, air-speed and glide-path, along with its airport database, to predict a potential conflict between the aircraft's flight path and the terrain. Even so, the pilot must memorise what immediate actions to take in case the aircraft suddenly gets trapped in a high-terrain area.

Here's what happened when a pilot forgot this important item. In December 1995, an American Airlines Boeing 757 was on a scheduled flight from Miami International Airport to Cali in Colombia but crashed into a mountain due to navigational error. Nine seconds before the plane hit the mountain, the Ground Proximity Warning System (GPWS, the early version of EGPWS) sounded the alarm, announcing an imminent terrain collision. The captain attempted to climb clear of the mountain. However, because the aircraft's 'spoilers' had earlier been deployed to increase rate of descent, they now reduced the climb-rate, and so the aircraft hit the mountain near its peak. Researchers have shown that had the Boeing pilot retracted the spoilers – part of the memory drills as on the Airbus – the aircraft would probably have cleared the terrain.

MEMORY ITEM NUMBER 4: HOW TO AVOID ONCOMING AIR TRAFFIC

The sky might seem like a very big space, but this is not

the case because of the spike in air travel in recent years, and for other technical reasons. Pilots get information of inadvertent traffic headed towards them from the Traffic Alert and Collision Avoidance System (TCAS), which can warn pilots if their planes are on a collision course and direct them on to a different path. The pilot must be able to swiftly follow TCAS directions without taking too long to digest the information.

In July 2002, a Russian Tupolev 154 collided with a Boeing 757 over Zurich due to pilot error. The TU154 crew had followed air traffic control's instruction to descend, but had continued to do so even after the TCAS advised them to climb.

Pilots are now trained to follow TCAS commands (which is a mandatory exercise during Base Checks). However, this may soon be scrapped as the technology is already in place for an automatic traffic avoidance system.

MEMORY ITEM NUMBER 5: THE PILOT(S) HAVE PASSED OUT! WHAT SHOULD WE DO?

As mentioned earlier, the general rule is that two pilots flying together should never eat the same food (especially seafood), and preferably should not eat at the same time either. In case of food poisoning, both pilots will be incapacitated, and the auto-pilot mode isn't yet smart enough to replace a human one unless in a prepared auto land.

Heart problems and fainting are generally the main causes of serious incapacitation. A pilot being incapacitated at a higher altitude is not as serious a situation as a pilot who's out for the count during the landing phase. In any event, a pilot must be healthy at all times in order to react immediately to such situations – needless to say, without referring to checklists or manuals.

MEMORY ITEM NUMBER 6: THE BRAKES DON'T WORK!
The loss of braking after touchdown is obviously an emergency situation. Fear not, for the memory drills for this are practised regularly by pilots.

MEMORY ITEM NUMBER 7: IT DOESN'T SEEM THAT FAST – UNRELIABLE AIRSPEED INDICATIONS
A failure to promptly recognise and respond to unreliable airspeed indications can result in loss of control of the plane. Briefly, airspeed is measured by comparing the difference between the air pressure sensed by the 'pitot head' or probe and static pressure at the 'static ports'. Complete or partial blockage of pitot heads and static ports due to ice, as experienced by Air France Flight 447, which crashed into the Atlantic Ocean in 2009, can confuse an unprepared crew. Hence the memory item for this is crucial in such an emergency.

MEMORY ITEM NUMBER 8: EMERGENCY DESCENT DUE TO LOSS OF PRESSURISATION

The air pressure inside the plane is higher than that outside of it, or the cabin air would be too thin to breathe in. At the first indication of a pressurisation problem, the flight crew must put on oxygen masks because pilots can lose consciousness in under a minute at high-altitude. It's imperative for flight crew to swing into action immediately; there's no time to look at the checklist.

What difference does this drill make? Here are two incidents; one where the emergency descent drill was promptly initiated and another where it was disregarded due to wrong diagnosis by the crew.

In April 1988, a Boeing 737 operated by Aloha Airlines experienced an explosive depressurisation and structural failure at 24,000 feet. Part of the cabin structure became detached from the aircraft during the flight. Despite this, the flight crew performed a successful emergency descent with only one fatality.

In August 2005, a Boeing 737 belonging to Helios Airways crashed in Greece following the incapacitation of the crew due to hypoxia or, lack of oxygen. The crew failed to detect the loss of pressurisation, and the failure to perform an immediate emergency descent led to the tragedy.

MEMORY ITEM NUMBERS 9 AND 10: WHAT IF THE AIRPLANE STALLS DURING TAKEOFF OR MID-FLIGHT?

'Stalling' can be quite a misleading and frightening term to the layperson. Non-pilots are familiar with what happens when a car engine stalls. Thus, the assumption is that when an aircraft stalls, the engine has quit and will be of no use for the rest of the flight. This, mercifully, is not true.

A stall, in aerodynamic terms, means that the wing has stopped producing lift because the critical angle of attack (the angle between the relative airflow and the axis of the wing) has been exceeded. This means that as the pilot slows down an aircraft, whether deliberately during training or accidentally due to a distraction, the necessary 'lift' to maintain the altitude is lost. If the angle of attack gets too high, the wing can no longer produce lift because the smooth flow of air over the wing is disrupted. As the wing loses its lift, the nose of the plane would generally drop if its centre of gravity is leaning forward. Then, the only way to resume normal flight is to reduce the angle of attack to re-establish proper lift. The plane will resume normal flight after recovery, unlike the dead engine of a stalled car.

So, a proper and fast technique (a memory item) to recover from a stall at takeoff and when cruising is crucial to prevent the plane from getting into trouble. The stall technique during the cruise was not properly executed on Air France Flight 447, which resulted in the loss of 228 lives.

The responsibilities of captain and first officer are heavy ones. This is why the 10 Memory Items are drilled into their very being, so that they can react immediately to untoward events.

ACKNOWLEDGING HUMANITY

Pilots are human and therefore, not infallible. Modern technology has made planes very safe today. The airline industry is, however, aware that human errors are a little more difficult to mitigate against. A captain is very mindful and during pilot briefings, he notices every detail that could potentially contribute to mistakes in the cockpit – a crew member who has quarrelled with his or her spouse before the flight, the one who is unwell or just looks flustered because he had to rush to avoid being late, and so on.

Briefings also cover safety aspects like the possibility of engine failure during take-off, or in case of technical abnormalities or bad weather. It's just like preparing for a road trip where you plan what to do if a cow wanders into your path while you're driving at high speed, or which direction to turn and what to do if you get a flat tyre.

So, you can imagine the amount of before-flight and landing briefings carried out on every route, day in and day out. That's how much pilots care for your safety and, of course, their own as they too have families to go home to. Sometimes though, for all the training in the world, a novel situation presents itself.

THE CURIOUS CASE OF THE CRIPPLED AIRBUS A380

Generally, most emergencies are textbook examples with procedures clearly laid out to ensure pilots know what to do in such instances. But there was an emergency over Singapore that was extraordinary and very difficult to handle.

On November 4, 2010, a Qantas Airbus A380 flying from Singapore to Sydney was hit by shrapnel from an exploding engine, and that caused extensive damage – the wing was punctured, part of its fuel system wrecked and one of its hydraulic systems disabled. The anti-lock brakes were also crippled and performance of engines numbers 1 and 4 were degraded. Moreover, the plane sustained damage to its landing flaps and the controls of its outer left engine.

As you can imagine, such a scenario could not have been foreseen or prepared for in training. But the captain, first officer and the additional three crew members in the cockpit pooled their resources and brought the plane down safely at Singapore's Changi Airport. Their skill, presence of mind and adaptability were a result of the rigorous pilot training,

When confronted with such a potential catastrophe, the captain's first priority is to determine whether it is feasible, legal and safe to land. The first officer has to furnish all the relevant information in aid of answering these questions, including if the runway is long enough to land based on the plane's system failures.

In the A380 accident, when the captain decided to turn back with his stricken plane, it was fortunate that the aircraft was close to Singapore, which has a 13,100-foot long runway. The supporting crew had to calculate the landing distance required based on the situation. Initially, feeding information on the failures and wet runway (a worst-case scenario) into the computer returned an invalid answer, meaning that it was literally impossible to land on the runway.

However, when it was ascertained that it was not raining in Singapore, the computer calculated a landing distance of 12,800 feet for dry runway conditions. This left a minimum margin of only 300 feet on Changi's 13,100-foot runway for the captain to play with.

Hypothetically, if the captain were to have landed the A380 on Sydney's longest runway (13,000 feet), he would only have had 200 feet to spare, but would've run out of runway space if he had tried to land on the longest runway (11,920 feet) at London's Heathrow. Had the captain elected to divert the plane to Kuala Lumpur International Airport, he would've had a longer runway (13,186 feet) at his disposal. Why would it take 12,800 feet for the plane to stop instead of half that distance? This was mainly due to the plane suffering damage so extensive that the landing flaps could not be deployed.

NOT JUST FLAPPING AROUND

Flaps are devices at the trailing edge of an airplane's wings that are used to either increase lift or drag, depending on pilot selection. The higher the flap selection is, the greater the drag (resistance).

Flaps are used when the aircraft has to slow down in preparation for landing. They are partially extended before takeoff to increase lift but are fully extended during landing to allow the aircraft to safely approach the runway at the lowest possible speed. Because the crippled A380 was unable to select full-flaps, it had to land at a higher speed, thus extending the landing distance to 12,800 feet.

As a result, the landing speed was 35 knots faster than a landing with full-flaps, causing four tyres to blow-out before the plane stopped completely – with 300 feet of runway to spare.

RADICAL WEIGHT LOSS

The A380 captain could have mitigated the extra landing distance by reducing the landing weight, which could have been achieved by dumping excess fuel.

On most commercial jet planes, take-off weights are always higher than the permissible landing weights for long-haul flights. On the Airbus A380, the maximum take-off weight is 574 tonnes but the maximum designed landing weight is only 391 tonnes. As such, the aircraft has to dump its excess fuel in order to land safely if an unplanned landing has to be carried out due to an emergency.

Some aircraft do not have the dumping function, such as the Airbus A320, and as such would need to burn off as much fuel as possible prior to landing. This happened in Los Angeles International Airport on September 21, 2005, when a JetBlue Airbus A320 suffered a nose landing-gear problem. The captain flew the plane in circles for more than two hours burning off fuel in order to lower the risk of fire upon landing.

As these examples show – there's no way a pilot can be *totally* prepared for every imaginable emergency but there are ways to significantly improve the odds when dealing with them. It has been statistically proven that preparation and training are paramount in successfully dealing with emergencies.

CHAPTER 4

PATIENCE, GRASSHOPPER
A pilot employs his skills as last resort

A superior pilot uses his superior judgment to avoid situations which require the use of his superior skill.

—**Frank Borman,** former astronaut

This quote says a lot about flying. What this means is that a good pilot has both good judgment and piloting skills, and the best way to improve his flying skills is by exercising good judgment first. Such a pilot would be able to make the right assessment and avoid risky action, instead of continuing with his decision in the face of circumstances.

If good judgment is so important, why have good piloting skills then, you may ask? Well, while it's important to have good judgment at all times, pilots too are human beings and can sometimes make mistakes. It's how quickly you rectify these mistakes that matters and, in this regard, good piloting skills help immensely.

HUMAN ERROR VERSUS MECHANICAL FAILURE

Some travellers fear flying because they're afraid the aircraft may not be able to physically withstand severe air turbulence, resulting in engines failing or wings snapping off. This, fortunately, is almost impossible. Modern planes are designed to be very reliable, practically 'un-crashable', as the latest advancements in aviation technology have reduced the odds of a major mechanical fault to a very negligible level.

On the other hand, it's harder to reduce human error where flying is concerned. The only way to do so is through rigorous training, which is the reason pilots have to pass base checks and practical exams every six months. This is to ensure pilots do not become complacent. The standard procedures and drills should be so well-ingrained that they become second nature should an emergency arise.

For example, Kathmandu in Nepal is a difficult destination for landing planes due to its location in the mountains nearly 4,400 feet above sea level. Airlines that wish to fly to Kathmandu first need to ensure that their pilots have received thorough training. They must be trained to overcome mechanical failure in bad weather, know how to execute an aborted landing and fly along escape routes between valleys. This will need to be done while relying purely on instruments, as they may not be able to see the whole route during bad weather.

TALKING LOUD AND CLEAR

There are times when accidents occur due to poor interaction between the captain and co-pilot. For example, when a captain makes a poor judgment and the co-pilot isn't assertive enough to speak up for fear of antagonising his superior, or when the captain refuses to pay attention to his co-pilot's advice.

In January 2004, a Boeing 737 crashed into the Red Sea because the captain was disorientated while flying at night and the co-pilot did not intervene quickly enough. This led to the loss of 148 lives.

In May 2010, the *Indian Bharat Chronicle* reported that the captain of a Boeing 737, who flew from Dubai to Mangalore, ignored his co-pilot's advice not to land at least twice. The warnings were in vain and the plane crashed and fell off the cliff from the table-top runway because of poor judgment. The aircraft had been coming in too fast and too high to land safely. This accident took 158 lives.

These mishaps have led to even more rigorous training that encourages co-pilots to be assertive and to intervene should the situation demand so.

GOOD JUDGMENT

Nowadays, instead of emphasising the pilot's skill in handling events like an engine failure on take-off (part of regulatory requirements), training is directed at coaching pilots to overcome seemingly common events that have often led to accidents. This way, the airline industry hopes that accidents due to human error will be greatly reduced. This is over and above International Civil Aviation Organization (ICAO)'s guidelines for Cockpit Resource Management (CRM) training that makes it mandatory for captains to listen to their co-pilots. While co-pilots may be less experienced, their opinions and judgments are just as valid.

There's a saying that goes: Good judgment comes from experience; experience comes from mistakes; and mistakes are often a result of bad judgment.

When can pilots safely see the result of their bad judgments and mistakes? Before they actually take to the skies, they practise (and practise) on a flight simulator, which enables them to learn what to do and what not to when flying an actual plane. If only life had the same training facility as a simulator! Read on...

CHAPTER 5

THE REALITY OF FLIGHT SIMULATION
Imagining virtually every possible scenario

Flight simulators play an integral part in honing a pilot's skills to fly passengers safely.

It was the first time I'd flown with a young female pilot. She had just graduated from a flying academy and showed some apprehension at being assigned to handle one of the most sophisticated cockpits – the Airbus A320.

"Captain, I'm not sure I can handle a plane with 180 passengers behind when I become a commander one day!" she said. I told her not to underestimate her own capabilities but to think positively and learn as much as she could.

It was years later when we met again. She was beaming with confidence, equipped with good technical knowledge and flying experience. About to become a commander, she was fully prepared to fly hundreds of passengers without any apprehension.

What makes a good captain? Extensive training in the flight simulator, for one. Through rigorous training and checks inside this 'box', pilots can continually hone and improve their handling skills to cope with all kinds of emergencies that arise in the course of flying.

Moore's Law, or the doubling of computing power every two years, means that planes are always being improved and made safer. But humans can't keep the same pace as machines, so trainers do their utmost to inculcate a Crew Resource Management (CRM) mentality in air crew to improve the human factor aspect, while pilots undergo all sorts of challenging exercises in the simulator.

WHEN WE USED TO DO IT FOR REAL

Good flying skills are developed by extensive use of flight simulators that can create myriad scenarios and crises in all the phases of flight, some of which a pilot will never encounter in his or her career. This is necessary because emergency situations are by definition unpredictable.

When I started flying many years ago, there were no flight simulators and simulating engine failure was done on real planes. It was a highly dangerous environment – more accidents were attributed to training than actual failures. Thankfully, such practices are now prohibited and are created in flight simulators instead.

Simulator training significantly reduces risk, saves time and money. For example, conducting various instrument approaches with different emergencies requires significant time spent repositioning the plane. However, in a simulator, as soon as one exercise is completed, the instructor can immediately reposition the plane to begin the next one just by touching the screen.

IF IT'S NOT ONE THING, IT'S ANOTHER.
THEN ANOTHER...

An airline assesses and monitors the proficiency of its pilots with what is called a Check Flight. A typical Check Flight comprises of critical exercises and usually begins with a rejected take-off. This is to hone a pilot's skill in making split-second decisions in a go or no-go situation. If a malfunction occurs below the 'decision speed' (this varies with the weight of the plane), it means the pilot must abort the take-off. If a failure happens after this speed, the plane must continue or end up crashing at the end of the runway.

Next, the examiner would simulate an engine failure either by a collision with a flock of birds or, an engine fire after take-off. This requires the pilot to correctly handle the failure, climb away and return for a safe landing or divert to a more suitable airport. On the return to land with the crippled plane, a further challenge is normally introduced, such as the need for an aborted landing to be carried out. This scenario can arise due to a blocked runway, instability suffered by the aircraft due to wind shear or when the pilot cannot see the runway due to low clouds.

The next sequence of the exercise involves putting the plane on a collision course with another. The examiner can vary the difficulty of the avoidance exercises with either one or two planes coming head-on.

Additionally, other major emergencies during the approach can include a pilot incapacitation exercise when the captain suffers a heart attack just before landing. The first officer would then immediately take over to abort or continue with the landing.

The flight simulator is a very versatile machine that can create all types of unique scenarios. Thunderstorms, patchy fog, slippery runway, blowing snow and multiple equipment failure can be created through the 'magic panel' at the back of the cockpit.

Emerging from the end of this four-hour training and check session every six months, the pilot is refreshed to handle the highly demanding job. If such an exercise was imposed on a driver every six months, I'm sure roads would be far safer for everyone.

NEW LESSONS FROM HISTORY

When an accident happens, simulators can be used to re-enact the flight conditions that led to the crash, based on the information found in the crashed aircraft's 'black box' or data-recording device. This helps identify what happened and pilots will learn how to overcome similar situations in the future. For example, there was speculation that the Air France Flight 447, which crashed into the Atlantic in 2009, may have encountered some kind of disturbance that created a 'jet upset' condition. This prompted the airline industry to look into this phenomenon to reduce future catastrophes.

Simulators are also used by some fear-of-flying clinics to systematically desensitise aviophobes. Participants are gradually exposed to their fear so they can learn to evaluate their situation logically and not emotionally. However, the success of such programmes depends on the participants and their willingness to overcome their fear of flying.

CHAPTER 6

THE GAMES WE PLAY

The pilots are out cold. Can you fly the plane?

Gamers and serious flight simulator enthusiasts often ask me if the hours they've spent flying a virtual plane means they can land a real airliner safely should the captain and co-pilot both become incapacitated.

While rare, such cases do happen, like Helios Airways Flight 522, where both pilots lost consciousness after failing to recognise a problem with the cabin pressurisation system. The plane eventually crashed into the side of a mountain because nobody knew how to get past the locked cockpit door to take control of the airplane. (Incidentally, the onboard computers flew the aircraft for about three hours unaided before it finally ran out of fuel.)

Movie plots involving aviation crashes sometimes give the impression that an ordinary passenger or cabin crew with no flying experience can help land a plane safely, perhaps with the assistance of someone from the flight tower over the radio.

Let's create a hypothetical scenario: Tom is a passenger who has absolutely no clue about flying; Dick, a newly qualified single-engine pilot with little flying experience; Harry plays flight simulators for hours on end; and Marvel is a fully qualified type-rated pilot who happens to be onboard while off-duty.

The first thing anyone needs to do before taking over would be to remove the incapacitated pilot from his seat. This would require a lot of strength and skill, as the seat belt would have to be removed and the pilot extricated from his seat properly so as not to accidentally hit any controls. Once that's been done, the question of who would be the most suitable candidate to take over becomes pertinent.

TOM, A PASSENGER WHO CAN'T FLY

Unlike a car, a commercial airliner is not an easy machine to handle for someone with no flying experience. First of all, Tom would need to get inside the cockpit and talk to someone over the radio. But he would need to know how to operate the radio on a Boeing or Airbus and which frequency to dial. This would probably be beyond the grasp of someone with no flying experience. Without help from an expert,

Tom would likely not even know where to begin. Not the best candidate for the job.

DICK, NOVICE PRIVATE PILOT LICENSE HOLDER

On the Helios flight, both pilots were incapacitated due to lack of oxygen from loss of cabin pressure. However, one flight attendant was still alive as he still had some oxygen from a portable bottle. He had some piloting experience just like Dick but he couldn't get through the locked cockpit door in time. Had the flight attendant been able to get into the cockpit, there might've been a chance he could have landed the aircraft using the automation with help from the ground.

The cause of the Flight 522 crash was the flight crew's failure to set the pressurisation switch correctly after maintenance. This allowed the plane to remain unpressurised until the cruise – similar to standing at the top of Mount Everest without any oxygen! If Dick is able to access the cockpit and communicate with the control tower, he might be able to land the plane safely.

HARRY, COMPUTER GEEK

A computer geek like Harry may have a better chance, provided he's used to flying a similar type of plane on his desktop simulator. This would require the autopilot to be still engaged, and the runway equipped with an Instrument

Landing System (ILS). It is also imperative that he be able to talk to another pilot over the radio. Unless these three basic requirements are satisfied, Harry would have some difficulty bringing the plane home safely.

The trick is for him to communicate his predicament over the radio and to keep the autopilot on. While it's possible to control the aircraft by selecting push buttons and turning knobs with instructions over the radio, flying manually by using the sensitive side-stick requires a lot of practice and skill.

As such, if Harry were to have the urge to hand-fly the plane, it would be a very difficult endeavour. Even professional pilots have to go through years of training and re-training in a full flight simulator to ensure they continue flying the plane safely all the time. However, a large airliner like an Airbus A380 could be landed using the autopilot without anyone having to touch the controls.

Given the right conditions – good weather, a perfect plane, Harry being familiar with the systems on that particular aircraft type and continuous assistance from a qualified pilot or instructor – he might be able to pull it off if he can keep his cool.

CAPTAIN MARVEL, OFF-DUTY PILOT

It is really quite unlikely that both pilots become incapacitated during a flight. The Helios disaster is a remarkable exception.

But there have been cases where one pilot of a smaller plane has been disabled, such as by a heart attack, and another non-pilot was able to safely bring down the plane.

On long-haul flights, pilot incapacitation isn't a major problem as most airlines would have two sets of crew (four pilots) onboard. On short-haul flights where there's only the captain and first officer, the two-pilot incapacitation issue, though still very remote, could pose some problems.

In such an instance, the flight attendant may have to page for any experienced pilot travelling onboard to help out. An off-duty pilot like Marvel would have the best chance at safely landing a stricken aircraft.

As you can see, not every Tom, Dick or Harry can easily land a plane without rigorous flight training and experience. That said, if you're an avid flight simulator player, your time spent playing the game would not go amiss should such a situation arise while you're onboard an aircraft. The scenario remains highly unlikely, but your knowledge can be useful as a last resort. Having Captain Marvel on the same flight would of course be the greatest help among all the others.

CHAPTER 7

IT WAS A DARK AND STORMY NIGHT
Don't mess with Mother Nature

The term 'typhoon' comes from the Chinese, and literally means 'big wind'. It's the same as cyclones and hurricanes, except it is known by different names in different parts of the world. In China, typhoons appear beginning May and last all the way until November, and are particularly prevalent during September. They're usually associated with strong winds and heavy rain.

Technically, a typhoon happens when surface winds reach more than 119kph, and even up to 249kph. More interestingly, it is also known as the 'divine wind'. How can something so destructive also be considered divine? In the thirteenth century, a typhoon destroyed an invading Mongol fleet in Japan. The storm was called 'kamikaze', meaning 'wind of the gods', so named because the Japanese emperor had prayed for divine intervention in the battle. 'Kamikaze' is of course most infamously associated with the suicide pilots of Japan in WWII. It was thought that they too were borne by the divine wind. So there you have it, a historical reason for the healthy respect pilots have for the power of the divine wind, or Mother Nature.

TRYST WITH A TYPHOON

I remember vividly an incident some years back in Shanghai when I refused to take off on a Boeing 777 because of an approaching typhoon. An irate passenger on my flight said something to the effect of, "How come the other foreign Boeing 777 pilot, flying the same aircraft from another airline was able to take off while this cowardly pilot refuses?" This remark prompted the airport manager to persuade me to take off. I was, however, adamant and told him, "No way, my friend!"

Naturally, I too was surprised that the Boeing 777 which was parked next to us took off. Of course, this angered the passengers who had been stranded in the lounge for several hours. It made plain sense to the passengers that if the other flight could take off, then I was just being difficult.

I had my reasons, and they were good ones too. You see, an approaching typhoon comes with winds gradually increasing in strength. More so, the wind on that day was blowing across the runway. Every plane has a crosswind limitation beyond which the manufacturer cannot guarantee a safe take-off. The wind on that fateful day was gusting well above the take-off limit, hence my refusal to take off and endanger the lives of those in my care.

WE DON'T NEED ANOTHER HERO

I tried my best to explain my refusal to take off to the sceptical manager, to no avail. However, all that changed when we overheard on the radio that a United Airlines Boeing 747 and a Virgin Atlantic Airbus A340 had been forced to return after aborting their departures.

I felt a sense of vindication that I'd stood firm in refusing to give in to the demands of the airport manager. My passengers' safety was of the utmost importance, and I was certainly not about to take any chances with it. A doctor once commented that my responsibility was heavier than his – when a doctor makes a mistake, only one patient dies, while a pilot's mistake would impact the lives of hundreds.

The other pilot may have been trying to be heroic but each time we pilots sign in to fly an aircraft we are duty-bound, morally and professionally, to operate the plane as safely as possible. In all honesty, I'd rather be a coward than a dead hero.

WET AND WILD

Typhoons come bearing more than just strong winds. They bring heavy rain too. A wet runway poses further problems to a landing aircraft due to the aquaplaning effect, where the tyre loses grip and starts skidding on the surface of the water. Aquaplaning, or hydroplaning, can reduce the effectiveness of wheel braking in aircraft on landing, which could cause it to veer off the runway. This can happen when an aircraft lands on a runway surface contaminated with standing water (a merely wet runway is okay). It can have adverse effects on ground controllability, as well as braking efficiency.

Flying an aircraft in the vicinity of a typhoon can also cause a lot of air turbulence. Your pilot knows how to conduct the plane and will immediately put in remedial measures in the event of a typhoon or similarly serious weather conditions. He'll make sure his route is at least off and away from the track of the typhoon. Pilots will also be notified of prevailing typhoons by the weather authority and the estimated time of the impact. Initially, the report will be given every 12 hours, with the interval shortened to six hours once the full force of the typhoon is on its way. All these, and the latest technological developments, help the pilot steer clear of typhoons so he can fly you to your destination in the safest and most comfortable manner.

SHAKEN, NOT STIRRED

Back to the cancelled Shanghai flight that I was flying: it was delayed until the typhoon passed the next day. The passengers who were initially very angry with us were soon grateful when they met us at the hotel lift. Many still looked pale and shaken even though they were safe in the hotel building; they'd felt the increasing strength of the gale force winds generated by the typhoon on the bus back to the hotel and realised the potential calamity they'd escaped and what untold misery could have ensued had their pilot insisted on being heroic instead of mindful of their safety.

Typhoons and other serious climatic conditions often cause disruptions to air traffic either because airports are closed or flights are cancelled. So please be patient if the captain announces that your flight has been delayed or cancelled, as getting you to your destination is no longer a priority and he is more concerned about your safety. You may arrive late but you may have also escaped a potentially dangerous situation.

MOTHER NATURE'S MOOD SWINGS

As each year-end approaches, while Santa Claus is busy preparing for his 'annual flight' around the world, pilots from tropical regions too get ready to face the snow as they fly towards the Northern Hemisphere.

Preparation is half the battle won; safety is so important that airlines proactively prepare their pilots by including a wintry scenario into their Check Flight syllabus. This is to ensure that all aircrew members are sufficiently trained to handle the hazards of winter operations if they encounter unpredictable cold weather events.

For a start, during training in wintry conditions, the runway surface can be simulated to be slippery, making braking action less effective. This is to highlight that a longer landing distance would be required in such conditions. Pilots under Check have to precisely calculate such details to ensure that safety performance is met. Otherwise, the landing would be aborted.

In January 1982, a World Airways DC-10 skidded off an icy runway at Boston International Airport when it touched down about half a mile off the landing point. The runway was covered in ice and braking action was poor. The pilot was not able to stop in time. The plane ended up in the icy waters of Boston Harbour with two fatalities out of the 210 passengers.

Two days before Christmas in 2009, a UK Ryanair Boeing 737-800 skidded off the runway at Prestwick Airport in Scotland after hitting a patch of ice after landing. Pilots are constantly reminded to taxi (move) very slowly on contaminated runways or taxiways. Once an aircraft starts to skid, a pilot can lose control of the plane easily.

So when it snows, runways are regularly cleared by ploughs to ensure that braking action is effective and safe, not only on runways but on taxiways as well. Besides the dangers of skidding, the captain must also remove any ice or snow (de-ice) accumulated on the aircraft before the plane departs an airport.

STAYING IN SHAPE

Do not be alarmed if you see vehicles circling the aircraft, spraying liquid on your plane on a wintry day. Normally, the captain keeps passengers informed of this procedure. The spray not only removes snow or ice but also prevents further build-up on the plane's wings. This is crucial for a safe take-off. Ice accumulation on the wings may change its shape and impair the lifting efficiency of the plane during takeoff. The effectiveness of this procedure depends on the prevailing temperature. The pilot must take off as soon as possible, before the hold-over time expires. (Hold-over time is the estimated time before the anti-icing spray loses its effect.)

On January 13, 1982 a Boeing 737 crashed after taking off in a snow storm from Washington National Airport due to ice accumulation on its wings. Only five of 79 people onboard survived.

A subsequent investigation determined that the crash had been caused by pilot error. The pilots had failed to switch on the ice protection system, induced more ice accumulation on the wings by using reverse-thrust to move the plane, and did not reject the take-off after sensing trouble. Due to the delay in departure, the effectiveness of the de-icing liquid was reduced but the captain decided not to return for a further reapplication to avoid further delay.

The pilots' decision to stick closely behind another jet in the mistaken belief that heat from the engines ahead would melt the snow and ice on the wings was also ill-calculated. In fact, this non-standard procedure actually aggravated the situation as the ice, instead of falling off the plane, refroze later.

The airline industry now practises Evidential Base Training (EBT) and learns from past mistakes, simulating similar adverse conditions during training to ensure pilots are aware of the pitfalls.

CLIMATE CHANGE

Mother Nature's increasingly frequent outbursts mean that pilots may have to deal with volcanic ash from eruptions.

Why does the airline industry need to take costly precautions in the face of such geographical activity? Well, safety is paramount in view of what volcanic ash can do to planes, as it did to a British Airways Boeing 747 in June 1982. The plane was flying from Kuala Lumpur to Perth but unwittingly went into an ash plume from an eruption southeast of Jakarta. The volcanic ash quickly accumulated in the engines, causing all four to flame-out.

Luckily, the plane was cruising at 37,000 feet and was able to glide out of the ash cloud after the engine failure. In fact, the crew calculated that without engines the plane would have been able to glide for about 23 minutes, or about 91 nautical miles, from 37,000 feet.

Fortunately, they were able to restart all four engines at a lower altitude after the molten ash solidified and broke off, although one failed soon after. Visibility was also severely limited as the cockpit windscreens had been badly sandblasted by the ash. The captain nonetheless managed to successfully land in Jakarta, relying only on instruments.

Seven years later, a KLM Boeing 747 en route to Narita (Tokyo) from Amsterdam suffered a similar fate. All four engines of the six-month-old plane failed but were restarted at 14,000 feet. It landed safely at Anchorage International Airport in Alaska. The plane had encountered the 'The Jakarta Effect'.

It was because of incidents like these that the airline industry took the drastic step of shutting down a massive part of European airspace in the spring of 2010, following the eruption of Eyjafjallajökull in Iceland.

This was also when the public felt most keenly how a week's loss of air transportation could so drastically disrupt lives and businesses. The ash plume cost the airline industry alone US$5 to 10 billion a week due to the grounding of flights.

Part of a pilot's pre-flight preparation is to be notified by the flight dispatch centre whether his route for the day would be affected by any volcanic activity, and if the flight will be rerouted to avoid passing through these dangerous areas.

Nevertheless, there are drills pilots follow in the unlikely event that they come into contact with volcanic ash plumes that linger high in the sky. Unfortunately, attempting to detect these plumes visually can be quite difficult as some are not easily visible and can only be identified by the presence of an acrid odour that smells like electrical smoke, burnt dust or sulphur.

If this situation arises, the first action is to do a 180-degree turn to avoid the possibility of engine failure. Yes! Chicken out, turn around and run for your life.

THE WIND BENEATH (ON TOP AND SIDEWAYS) YOUR WINGS

Wind can be good, bad or ugly depending on its direction relative to the plane. Tail-wind is good when it helps to speed up a long journey but bad during a landing as it can cause the landing distance to be longer, thus reducing the safety margin. Sometimes it may even cause a tail-strike, where the bottom of the plane scrapes the runway. Conversely, a headwind, or wind blowing from the front, is good on take-off or landing as a shorter runway is required but bad on long flights as it slows the plane down.

On take-off, a strong headwind gets the plane airborne faster compared to a tailwind. As such, air traffic controllers will use the runway with the strongest headwind. Consequently, some delays are to be expected when there is a need to change runways due to the shift in wind direction, as all planes would have to be re-sequenced either on the ground or in the air for safety reasons.

Wind can be ugly when it blows across the runway at speeds beyond the limitations imposed by plane manufacturers. This is known as cross-wind. For instance, on an Airbus A330, when the wind exceeds about 40 knots, landing is not allowed on a dry runway. In wet conditions, the cross-wind limit is reduced to 27 knots as it's more difficult to keep aircraft centred on a slippery runway.

In August 22, 1999, a China Airlines MD-11 flight to Hong Kong crashed due to a strong crosswind. Strong crosswind landings may be a little difficult as the nose has to be pointed into the crosswind to maintain the centreline of the runway. It looks awkward as the plane has to 'crab-in', with the nose pointing back to the runway centre-line just before touching down.

In the China Airlines accident above, the captain landed hard on the right-side landing gear. As a result, the right engine scraped the runway causing the right main landing gear and the wing on that side to break off. The plane then rolled inverted as it skidded off the runway.

There are lessons to be learned by pilots to never land or take off when the crosswind is beyond the manufacturer's recommended limitations.

THE VICIOUS WIND

A report speculates that wind shear was the probable cause of a Boeing 737 crashing into the sea at Bali International Airport on April 13, 2013. Luckily, all 101 passengers and seven crew survived the crash even after the plane broke in half in shallow waters.

Severe wind shear can be very vicious. It's caused by a sudden, powerful change in wind direction that occurs frequently in or near thunderstorms. The downdraft created can give rise to a strong headwind that will cause a corresponding increase in airspeed. When a plane passes through the downdraft, it encounters a tailwind which can cause the aircraft to dangerously lose airspeed and altitude.

Airplanes are most vulnerable to wind shear during take-offs and landings, and the situation can turn very ugly if the pilot is caught by surprise. It's caused several crashes.

On June 24, 1975, an Eastern Air Lines Boeing 727 crashed while landing at JFK International Airport in New York due to severe wind shear caused by thunderstorms. Only 11 of the 124 people on board made it. A subsequent investigation found that the captain was aware of reports indicating severe wind shear on the approach path but decided to continue nonetheless. It was a fatal decision.

On August 7, 1975, a Continental Airlines Boeing 727 taking off from Denver International Airport in Colorado crashed due to severe wind shear. The 134 people aboard the aircraft survived the crash, although 15 were seriously injured. The aircraft was badly damaged.

On July 3, 1982 a Pan-Am Boeing 727 crashed on take-off after encountering wind shear. The aircraft was destroyed during the impact and subsequent ground fire, with many fatalities.

THIS WEATHER FORECAST COULD SAVE YOUR LIFE

But you shouldn't worry; improvements in technology have come to the rescue. Human beings are very innovative. Lessons from past accidents always help to make flying safer in the future.

Wind shear detection technology has been developed to allow pilots to predict wind shear even before takeoff, and most modern aircraft are now installed with this system. This warning system makes use of the weather radar to identify wind shear before takeoff. The radar picks up water and ice particles ahead of the airplane and warns the pilot with an audio message: "Wind shear ahead!" This is effective and gives the pilot an opportunity to abort the take-off.

While airborne, during take-off or landing, this system also warns of any wind shear. It's not clear whether the wind shear warning was activated in the 2013 Boeing 737 accident in Bali. Since the installation of this warning system, I've only encountered a real wind shear warning once in my career, during my approach to land. I did what I was taught – abort the landing and return for another safe one only when wind conditions had subsided.

The next time you see a plane landing cocked, that is, pointing into the direction of the wind and not on the runway centre-line, you know the captain's working very hard to control a cross-wind landing. He has to do that 'crabbing' manoeuvre or miss aligning on the runway centre line. Not to worry though. Just before touchdown, he'll use the rudder to bring the plane towards the centre. With that in mind, I hope you can breathe easily on future plane rides.

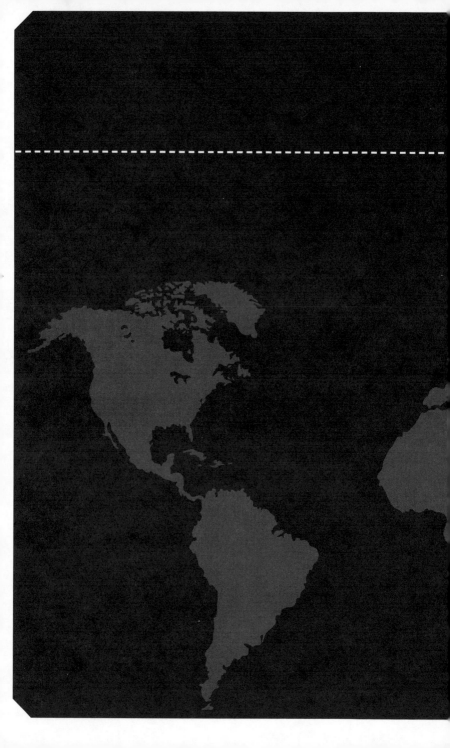

PART II

FASTEN YOUR SEATBELTS:
IT'S TIME TO TAKE OFF

CHAPTER 8

THINGS THAT GO BUMP ON THE FLIGHT
Turbulence, wings and related things

I often get e-mails from passengers with amusing anecdotes. Sometimes, as with inflight stories (or any fishing tales, for that matter) these stories have to be taken with a pinch of salt.

One guest wrote to me about her mother's 'scary' experience on a recent flight, where the plane faltered and the engines went 'clunk-clunk-clunk' before the plane dived 'hundreds of feet' with people screaming, crying and praying. Although this does sound like a scary scenario, before you get unduly alarmed, I'd like to explain what really happened on this flight to put your mind at ease.

In this case, the plane had encountered very bad turbulence as it was flying in the vicinity of a typhoon. Naturally, it was neither a comfortable nor pleasant experience. Nevertheless, turbulence is not to be feared, as long as one's seatbelt is securely fastened. When properly buckled up, flying during turbulence is not an issue of safety but rather one of discomfort.

In turbulence, the plane is normally flying on autopilot. It pays to remember that during the cruise, you are moving at about 800 feet per second or around 540 mph. To give you a better idea, that's whizzing along three football fields, each about 300 feet in length, in one second – that's three Wembley Stadiums every second.

Now, imagine the air over the first football field is flowing downwards, while the air over the next field is flowing upwards. This is followed by the air going down again over the third field. On a jet, you'll be pushed up for one-third of a second, then you're over the second field where downward-moving air pushes down on the plane for another third of a second. Then you're over the third field and move up for the last third of that second.

So there really isn't much time to go up or down, and the plane generally stays at its assigned altitude unless the autopilot is tripped by very severe turbulence. This can be manually over-ridden though, and the captain can easily regain control. The drop you feel is actually minimal because you go from downward-moving air to upward-moving air so quickly that neither has time to do much. You simply feel it as a jolt because you're hitting the bump incredibly fast.

NONE MORE TERRIFYING

The terror that passengers experience is normally created by their imagination – they imagine falling hundreds of feet but the altimeter in the cockpit shows otherwise. There's no way for a passenger to know how much the aircraft has dropped, or 'dived', unless the plane is equipped with Air Show or video screens.

As for the clunking sound, it doesn't indicate that the engine is faltering but rather that the pilot is reducing the speed of the plane, just like how you would slow down on approaching a speed bump on the road.

IS THAT A HOLE IN THE SKY?

On a flight home from London to Kuala Lumpur, I was tossed around in a sleeping bunk by severe turbulence while my relief crew flew the plane. That sudden mid-air upheaval reminded me that I was flying over the Bay of Bengal and that it was time to resume my shift.

Air turbulence can be very scary for first-time fliers. These free but unexpected roller coaster rides on a plane are rarely explained by most pilots. Some passengers will feel that the plane is flying into an 'air pocket', a vacuum in the sky that causes it to fall from the sky or drop hundreds of feet,but there's no such thing as an 'air pocket'. The term was mistakenly coined by a journalist during WWI to describe air turbulence. The expression caught on and continues to be misused today. One traveller claimed that he actually experienced dropping 'thousands of feet' in an 'air pocket'. Although it is possible to lose some height, it's actually impossible to fall thousands of feet from a hole in the sky because there's always air in the atmosphere to hold up the plane.

From experience, a plane rarely suffers a dramatic drop in altitude in turbulence unless caught in a bad downdraft. In fact, modern planes are usually on autopilot during a normal cruise and this system electronically locks on the altitude and set-course unless the autopilot is tripped.

You may be jostled around in the plane, but normal turbulence does not affect the altitude much. That's just the perception of anxious passengers; the plane really hasn't lost much altitude. Most seasoned passengers don't even raise an eyebrow during a bumpy ride; they know there will be turbulence that when storm clouds are present. Strong winds and thunder clouds are easily observed and experienced pilots know how to handle them well.

TRICKSY CLOUDLESS SKIES
That said, even experienced pilots may find it difficult to avoid 'clear-air turbulence' at times, which occurs even in cloudless skies. Pilots try their best to avoid flying through

areas of known turbulence but this is not always possible because heavy air traffic does not allow an alternative level or if the poor weather is too widespread.

Unfortunately, on long-haul flights, it is impossible to totally avoid turbulence. While pilots try their best to steer clear of environmental conditions that cause turbulence by deviating from the route or climbing and descending, sometimes, we're still caught by turbulence that isn't easily observable.

IF IT ROCKS, ENJOY THE RIDE

Once, on a flight from London to Kuala Lumpur, I rerouted 150 nautical miles off the original route that would have crossed a huge thunderstorm in the Bay of Bengal, and we were still affected by the turbulence, albeit at much reduced intensity. But when I checked with my senior flight attendant in the cabin, she reported that most of my passengers had slept throughout the rocking motion!

Moderate turbulence is something that a traveller has to live with for some time until better technology can eliminate or reduce this effect significantly. Until then, please remember that turbulence a pilot can fly through is nothing to be concerned about. It's generally an issue of discomfort rather than one of safety as long as you have your seat belt securely fastened.

WINGING IT

Here's another worry of newbie travellers: will the wings snap off in heavy turbulence? Just how resilient are they? So far, there's only been one such recorded case: A commercial plane, an old Boeing 707, encountered extreme turbulence and crashed near Mount Fuji in Japan in 1966. The jolt imposed a force in excess of the designed limit of the vertical stabiliser (tail-fin) but not on the wings.

However, the structure of a modern aircraft is incredibly strong. Take for instance the Boeing 777. During development, the wings were thoroughly tested to see if they could survive the strongest force that turbulence and bad handling would produce in flight.

The engineers subjected the Boeing 777 to up to 150 per cent of the strongest force possible to see if it would break apart. Then, during the full-scale destruct test, they had the wings pulled 24 feet above their normal position before they actually broke.

Engineers used computer-controlled hydraulic actuators to apply about half-a-million pounds of pressure on each wing until both broke at the predicted position. This confirmed that the plane's wings could withstand the load it was designed for.

Safety authorities in Europe also ensure that very stringent rules are applied when designing wings on all modern Airbus aircraft.

A HEALTHY ROAR

Clear-air turbulence, which occurs in fair weather, is difficult to always see or predict, so I often advise my passengers to fasten their seatbelts even when the seatbelt sign is off. This is also in compliance with the advisory by the FAA (Federal Aviation Authority of the US) to all airlines urging the use of seat belts at all times when passengers are seated as a precaution against unexpected turbulence.

Remember, pilots don't like turbulence too and we'll take any and all precautions to avoid them whenever possible. If we can't avoid it, we'll do everything possible to mitigate the effects (such as switching on the seatbelt sign and reducing the speed of the plane). As the plane slows down, the computer sends a signal to bring the power back, a function of the automatic thrust system. So don't be alarmed by the engines sounding different. I once had to calm a fearful flyer who asked whether the engines were failing since the sound of the engines had changed.

So don't worry about turbulence when you next encounter it. Just fasten seat belts and pretend you're on a roller coaster or a boat in choppy waters!

IF YOU'RE HEARING THINGS...

Do you find the lights, sounds and sensations during a flight worrying? No fear, I'll explain.

IS THERE A POOR DOG LOOKING FOR ITS OWNER?

Once you've settled down comfortably in an Airbus A320, you may hear the sound of a 'dog' barking from below, in the cargo bay, as soon as one of the engines starts. Is that someone's lost pet? No, it's the hydraulic power transfer unit (PTU) coming into operation and doing a self-test.

It arises when the PTU is transferring hydraulic pressure from one side to the other. This automatic transfer provides the power required as backup for the many safety functions necessary in an emergency. If one engine fails, this ensures that there is sufficient hydraulic power to stop the plane or assist the lowering of the landing gears and flaps for a safe landing.

WHY HAS IT GONE QUIET?

As you get airborne, the thundering engine noise appears to reduce in intensity, and you may feel as though the plane is sinking. This is because pilots must now be mindful of noise pollution especially for nearby residents on the ground, such as in the London city area. Pilots will begin what is known as Noise Abatement Procedures where they have to reduce engine power at around 1,000 feet after takeoff in order not to 'ring the bells' or trigger alarms below.

If not, the roaring engines would activate the sensitive equipment on the ground that record noise levels, resulting in airlines being fined. It's very much like how drivers get fined for exceeding the speed limit, only this infringement costs much more. This procedure is not only practised at major airports but during almost every departure today.

WHY DO I HAVE A SINKING FEELING...

This sensation is perceived only by some, especially first-time flyers. The motion arising from the thrust reduction causes a stimulation of the inner ear, which in turn disturbs your sense of balance and equilibrium. This is especially pronounced in an enclosed area of the airplane cabin as you have no visual reference to the outside environment. It immediately creates a sensation as if you are sinking rather than climbing. So, fret not the next time you experience it during takeoff – it's nothing to worry about.

...AND AM WORRIED WE MIGHT BE STRUCK BY LIGHTNING?

While there were initial suspicions that lightning may have caused the Air France Flight 447 disaster, this was proven untrue following the retrieval of the black box some two years after the crash.

Lightning, though fearsome, is not exactly dangerous to airplanes. Even a direct strike would not penetrate the cabin or affect the engines and fuel tanks. In fact, statistics have shown that, on average, an airplane is struck by lightning at least once a year, some more frequently, and others not at all, with little or no adverse effects.

When a plane is struck by lightning, the electrical charge merely traverses the length of the aircraft and exits harmlessly through the static wicks at the trailing edges of the flaps or tail. The next time you happen to sit by a window seat behind the wings of a Boeing 737, have a look for these static wicks – they look like tiny paint brushes with fine hairs sticking out at the end of the flaps. On the Airbus A320, they look like antenna-like rods.

The strike may cause some small burn marks on the fuselage skin at the point of impact. The pilot would normally be aware of such a strike and will report this incident to the engineers after landing for further inspection and rectification if necessary.

WHY THE MOOD LIGHTING IN THE CABIN BEFORE TAKE-OFF AND LANDING?

For safety reasons, as with so many other things about flying. In the unlikely event of an emergency evacuation, your eyes need to be fully adapted to the light values of the night so that you can safely jump out of the plane onto the slides. In an emergency, every second counts. Similarly, pilots are told to switch on all internal cockpit lighting when flying in the vicinity of lightning. This is to prevent the intense brightness of nearby lightning flashes from blinding them by ensuring their eyes are acclimatised to light.

I hope I've been able to put to rest some of the common worries about flying by explaining what happens in an aircraft during flight. As the American poet and philosopher Ralph Waldo Emerson once said, 'Knowledge is the antidote to fear.'

CHAPTER 9

NOW SCREENING

Not your usual inflight movie

In the name of security, the nature of the flying experience for the traveller has changed quite a bit since the glamour days of the jet-setter. A passenger on one of my flights became very upset when he wasn't allowed to visit and view the cockpit, claiming that it was allowed in his country. He was politely told that such practices were banned after the September 11 attacks.

Airline security is now more stringent than it has ever been. The passenger would be reassured that it wasn't him that was the problem; pilots too are subject to security procedures. On one flight operating out of Dubai, I was subjected to an incredibly thorough security check, more so than many of my passengers. I had to go through the screening machine, had my laptop checked twice (while switched on and off), was given a pat-down, and had my jackets and shoes removed for inspection. Imagine that! Many would think that as a captain flying a Boeing 777 to New York, what harm could I inflict?

The airport authorities refused to take any chances and were merely doing their job in ensuring all procedures were adhered to before the crew and passengers were allowed onboard. Where air security is concerned, it's better to be safe than sorry.

What's the rationale behind the inconvenience that mars what used to be a gracious way to travel? It's true that frequent flyers are incensed by security screenings at major international airports, from full-body scanning machines to physically intrusive pat-downs; they're seen as an invasion of privacy and an outrage of modesty.

Security authorities say that only a small percentage of air travellers undergo the physical pat-down or full-body scanning. They claim both procedures can effectively detect hidden weapons and explosives. These few extra safety precautions, no matter how inconvenient to passengers, can save lives and are widely considered to be foolproof.

Full-body scanning involves the use of advanced imaging technology. One common concern about such technology is whether it has harmful effects, especially on unborn children. Current expert evidence states that full-body scanning is safe for all, including children, pregnant women and even individuals with medical implants.

In fact, the screening process meets all health and safety standards, with health authorities confirming that the radiation projected on screened individuals falls far below standard dosage limits. The energy projected is many thousand times less than that transmitted by a mobile phone.

DRESSED TO KILL

Why was I made to take off my shoes for inspection before proceeding to my plane and then to New York? This stringent measure was put in place after a passenger by the name of Richard Reid made an attempt to cause damage to a Boeing 767 flying from Paris to Miami on December 21, 2001.

According to reports, Reid was wearing shoes that had been remodelled to hide plastic explosives in hollowed out soles. If detonated, the explosives could easily have blown a gaping hole in the fuselage of the aircraft. Reid had attempted to detonate the explosives but his efforts were foiled by the quick-thinking crew and passengers.

In another incident in 2009, a passenger onboard flight 253 from Amsterdam to Detroit was found to have explosives sewn onto his underwear. The explosives failed to detonate properly and the accused was badly burnt in the process. If it had exploded as planned, one can only imagine the number of fatalities. The incident could have been averted if the screening process was thorough and mandatory.

SHOPPING CAN BE INFLAMMATORY

Travellers are also often annoyed by the ban on carrying onboard liquids, aerosols and gels (LAGS) exceeding 100ml. Security officials have uncovered plots to cause severe damage to aircraft and loss of life by using liquid explosives. This particular plot involves carrying liquid explosives disguised as beverages or other common objects such as toiletries and even baby formula in carry-on luggage.

Binary explosives, which are created by combining two volatile liquids together, are a major cause for concern for security officials. They may look fairly harmless but can potentially cause catastrophic damage when mixed together. So if security personnel tell you to bin the water bottle or cream that exceeds 100ml, don't argue and follow the rules. They're merely making sure that everyone flies safely. Stringent screening procedures and checks on LAGs are admittedly a hassle for travellers and complicate duty-free shopping. However, this inconvenience is worth the trouble if it offers you real peace of mind.

HI, JACK!

A word of caution: Security officers at airports have no sense of humour when the safety of people and planes are at stake. Do not even think of cracking jokes about weapons, bombs or terrorist threats in the airport or plane. This is a serious matter and you could potentially be jailed even for a seemingly harmless joke.

In September 2011, a woman thought it funny to play a joke by sticking a drawing of a bomb with the word 'boom' on her friend's suitcase. This led to the entire terminal being shut down for nearly two hours, forcing several planes to be re-routed to other airports until the bomb squad and sniffer dogs finished sweeping the building for explosives.

So, if you think of a really funny joke about bombs just as you're about to board an airplane, for your own safety, keep it to yourself until you've landed *and* are safely outside the airport! And no matter what, do not say 'Hi, Jack!' to a fellow passenger on the flight – even if that's his name!

On one flight, a passenger told the security officer that he knew he was going to set off the metal detector because he had a metal pin in his hip. He hoped the officer would be less strict and let him through without any additional screening. Luckily, the security officer followed the standard guidelines and patted him down. Guess what turned up? A gun strapped to the passenger's leg.

CHAPTER 10

ARE WE THERE YET?
Not so fast. Here's why.

Aircraft captains are required to carry out a thorough physical inspection of their planes for every flight before take-off even if the aircraft has been certified fit for flight by an engineer.

If you're observant, you'll see a pilot in his safety jacket circling the plane on the tarmac performing an inspection while you're waiting in the departure lounge to board. The pilot is doing the so-called 'kicking the tyre and lighting the fire' ritual, as referred to by some military aviators – the normal pre-flight check, over and above the engineer's certification of fit-to-fly.

Some passengers get very upset when the captain announces that the plane has been delayed due to technical reasons. This, however, needs a little explanation. Modern aircraft have been built to be as reliable as possible; a plane undergoes thorough testing and is fitted with redundancy systems to allow it to proceed with the flight safely, even with minor defects. Severe defects, on the other hand, can prevent a plane from taking off unless the problem is rectified.

Despite the precautions, even the most advanced aircraft can still suffer from severe problems, such as damage to one of four jet engines in mid-air. That may sound scary but planes these days can fully cope with such a loss and can carry on flying with just the remaining three engines.

So if you ever find yourself waiting for a departure that's been delayed for technical reasons, be patient and remember the saying: Better late than never. The airline has your safety in mind and is doing everything it can to make sure the aircraft is in good working condition.

Sometimes, it is hard to produce a good enough explanation to explain why flights are delayed for irate passengers. However, the occasional delay is part and parcel of air travel. Mechanical problems are a common cause, aggravated by congestion resulting from crowded skies as more people are travelling by air. This explosion in air travel inevitably leads to late air-traffic clearance or planes being put on hold at the embarkation gate due to the many others queuing to fly out.

Pilots or airlines do not deliberately delay flights despite what passengers may think. Any delay – even for just a minute – has to be explained in detail by the captain. This shows how dedicated the airlines are in ensuring you depart on time. With that in mind, it is hoped that passengers can help airlines reduce delays and make flying safer and more comfortable for all.

TOO TERRIFIED TO FLY

Sometimes flights are delayed by the passengers too terrified to fly. On one flight out of London, a hysterical passenger insisted on being offloaded after the plane had departed the gate. Returning to the aerobridge is a time-consuming process and may result in the plane missing its slot to take off, forcing it to queue for a later departure.

Another fearful flyer once wrote to me saying that she was so scared of flying that she had not slept for two weeks. She suffered from palpitations and backaches because her muscles would tense up at the mere thought of flying. Another passenger wrote in asking for advice, as she couldn't eat for a week before her flight and cried herself to sleep thinking awful thoughts.

My response to all such travellers is to try to keep things in perspective. Everything we do in life involves some degree of risk. Walking across the street, driving to the supermarket, taking a shower at home – the list goes on. Although there is some risk in flying, air travel is still one of the safest modes of transport. Frankly, I'm more fearful of driving to work than sitting in a plane!

DELAYED BY... BAGGAGE

If a passenger with no checked-in baggage fails to turn up on time for the flight, he'll be left behind. But on international flights, a passenger who has checked-in with bags but fails to show up at the gate creates a bigger problem. The flight cannot depart until the bags are offloaded, in case they contain harmful contents that may endanger the aircraft during flight. If the captain ignores this to avoid the delay, he would be infringing on strict rules (Annex 17 of ICAO) leading to severe consequences for the pilot and the airline:

> Should passengers flying internationally with checked-in baggage fail to arrive at the departure gate before the flight is closed, that person's baggage must be retrieved from the aircraft hold before the flight is permitted to take off.
>
> —**International Civil Aviation Organisation**

The objective of this rule is to ensure passengers board flights onto which they have checked in their baggage. The general security presumption is that most terrorists would not want to kill themselves, and will not board an aircraft if they have placed an explosive in their baggage.

To achieve compliance, baggage is loaded manually into the cargo hold, with each item tagged during the process. The other parts of the baggage tags, which are bar-coded, are stuck onto a sheet and compared to a list of the passengers onboard. When a passenger with a checked-in bag fails to show up, baggage handlers will remove the piece of luggage belonging to that passenger. As you can imagine, depending on where the pieces of luggage are in the aircraft, this may take a lot of time and can cause major delays to the departure.

BLOWN UP MID-AIR

Unaccompanied bags containing explosives have led to the destruction of two planes in mid-air. On June 23, 1985, an Air India flight operating on the Montreal-London-New Delhi route exploded over Irish airspace. Investigators found that one of the passengers had checked-in a bag which contained explosives at Vancouver International Airport but failed to board the plane. All 329 people onboard died.

On December 21, 1988, a Pan-Am Boeing 747 was also torn apart by explosives, killing 243 passengers and 16 crew members on board. Eleven people on the ground at Lockerbie, Scotland, where the wreckage landed, also perished, bringing the total number of fatalities to 270.

Hopefully, this information goes some way towards making you feel less irritated with the pilots if you ever hear an apologetic voice informing you of a flight delay.

CHAPTER 11

BEST SEATS IN THE HOUSE
Some hotter than others

The captain sees a lot but can't possibly see it all. So the cabin crew are only too happy to relay little episodes of human life to me. I'd like to share some of them with you so you'll understand why the crew, or even pilots, may sometimes make seemingly unusual requests – like making you move from the seat of your choice on a flight that's not exactly full.

But first, where best to sit? Some say the best and safest seats are at the back of the aircraft. However, if you're prone to motion sickness during turbulence, then sit as close as possible to the wings, or at least in the area in front of the wings. This will put you closer to the plane's centre of gravity. Imagine yourself on a see-saw, the closer you are to the fulcrum of a see-saw, the more stable your position; similarly, the further you are from it, the more you are going to experience turbulence.

Seats near the rear of the aircraft tend to be a little noisier because you are at the back of the engine. Additionally, the effects of turbulence are more pronounced at the rear. Moreover, an added disadvantage with seats at the back is that you usually end up being the last to exit the plane. If you're in a hurry, you're in danger of missing a connecting flight.

'YOU REALLY SHOULDN'T BE SITTING HERE, MA'AM.'

A flight attendant told me about a very agitated passenger who wanted to know why he wasn't allowed to sit near the front when so many seats were available. (This happened during the free-seating era.) She was quite upset because the passenger had used very foul language when communicating with her. There are usually very few rude passengers but many flight attendants have nonetheless mastered the art of calming passengers and 'de-escalating' hostility. This is an essential skill to ensure the flight is conducted safely and without disruption to other passengers.

In truth, the first few rows at the front are sometimes kept vacant for load and balancing purposes, especially on light flights. As a boatman knows the importance of balancing for stability, an airplane too has to be well-balanced in order to fly safely. It is the job of the captain to ensure that this balance is maintained when boarding passengers.

Theoretically, a single passenger moving up and down the aisle could tip the aircraft nose up and down very slightly while it's cruising in the air. But in reality, modern planes have a built-in safety buffer to compensate for this – computers offset the imbalances by making slight adjustments to the power or control surfaces.

However, if the airplane is really off-balance, pilots would have a harder time dealing with the situation. For example, planes that are very tail-heavy may experience handling difficulties during the approach to land, potentially leading to a tail-strike.

Of course, the plane doesn't just have to be well-balanced; it also cannot be overweight. On one flight by an airline out of Chicago many years back, the captain reported that he needed more power and a longer distance to lift off the runway than he had expected. Upon investigation, it was found that the problem arose because most of the passengers onboard the flight were coin collectors. They were travelling to a convention and were carrying more than a tonne in coins in their carry-on baggage! And now, for a slightly controversial question.

WHO SHOULD SIT NEAR THE EMERGENCY EXITS?
Not a child, disabled person or senior citizen. Instead, these seats should only be occupied by 'able-bodied men'. Before

I'm accused of being politically incorrect, this translates as, any passenger who is best able to assist with the opening of the exits during an emergency.

In an emergency evacuation, Federal Aviation Administration regulations stipulate that the cabin should be fully evacuated in 90 seconds. Passengers who don't meet the definition of 'able-bodied men' would create an obstruction to quick evacuation. That said, passengers who need help evacuating will eventually be assisted by the crew once the main rush is over.

And what if a passenger seated nearest the exit won't cooperate? One day, the senior flight attendant came to me in the cockpit, desperately looking for help as a gentleman and his handicapped partner steadfastly refused to budge from seats nearest the emergency exit when requested to do so. (It's understandable why they would prefer them as the seats were more spacious and offered more legroom.)

I informed the flight attendant to politely relay the message that the flight would not take off unless they moved to other seats. Failure to do so would require me to seek assistance from security. That solved the problem quickly enough as they swiftly moved to different seats, worried that they might arouse the ire of the other passengers for delaying the flight. This was one episode that definitely tested the flight attendant's skills at diplomacy.

IT'S CALLED AN EMERGENCY EXIT FOR A REASON

Once, while scanning through the cockpit instruments for the door closed indications prior to departure, I saw something unusual – a caution light alerting me that someone was opening the emergency exit door.

I immediately called my senior flight attendant to find out what had triggered the warning. He confirmed that a mischievous passenger was playfully testing the emergency exit handle and ended up opening the door. The passenger, who occupied the seat next to the emergency exit, had been briefed earlier to act as the 'able-bodied man' to assist in opening the door in the event of an evacuation. But he wasn't to open it at any other time.

The flight attendant gently cautioned the passenger who then sat down meekly while we completed boarding and took off with the emergency exit door firmly secured. And this little anecdote neatly brings us to the following questions.

CAN THE CABIN DOORS BE OPENED IN FLIGHT?

A fearful flyer once asked me if the doors of the plane can be opened during flight should a passenger be mad enough do so. The answer is no.

The smaller emergency exits are prevented from opening during flight by the outward-pushing forces of the pressurised cabin. These doors are like drain plugs that open inward and no one would be able to overcome these forces until the plane is depressurised. In the case of the larger cabin doors, they are safely secured by a series of locks that are subjected to similar outward-acting pressure that prevents any attempt to open them.

Although it's impossible to open the cabin doors during a flight, I wouldn't suggest anyone mess around with the door handles as it would not only be futile, but you would be answerable to security when you arrive at the destination.

UNDER PRESSURE

A jet plane is designed to cruise at a high altitude to save fuel. However, flying high comes at a cost – lack of oxygen. To ensure there's sufficient oxygen for the passengers to breathe at such heights, the cabin must be pressurised.

Very simply, as the plane climbs, the air becomes thinner and the amount of oxygen decreases. So when the cabin is pressurised as the plane climbs it has the effect of squeezing the air back together, recreating the denser oxygen-rich conditions found closer to the ground. For example, when the Airbus A320 is in flight, the cabin altitude is set automatically near to around 2,500 feet when you are at 25,000 feet and 6,500 feet when the plane is actually at 35,000 feet.

Pressurisation also makes flying more comfortable as it allows for the gradual equalisation of your ears as the plane ascends to cruising altitude.

WHAT HAPPENS IF THE AIR GOES OUT...

In July 2008, a Qantas Boeing 747 flying from London to Melbourne suffered depressurisation when, according to investigators, an exploding oxygen bottle probably ripped a hole the size of a mini-van on the right side of its body, forcing it to make an emergency descent from 29,000 feet to 10,000 feet near Manila.

Pilots are well-trained in emergency descent procedures. It takes about five minutes to descend from 35,000 feet to 10,000 feet where oxygen is no longer required. The oxygen from your drop-down mask will last approximately 15 minutes so you'll have about 10 minutes to spare.

That said, please pay careful attention to the emergency demonstration, especially on the use of oxygen masks that will drop from the ceiling during an emergency descent. This is very important as it could save your life and those of the people around you.

CHAPTER 12

WE'RE THERE ALREADY?

The opposite of delay

Sometimes, you get there before you know it. How can this be so? Some hardened travellers might regard early arrivals as a minor miracle. Let's begin with knots. Traditionally, how fast an airplane flies is measured in knots. A knot is equal to one nautical mile per hour. One nautical mile is equal to 6,080 feet, longer than the statute mile used on the ground, which is equal to 5,280 feet.

Why are knots used to measure speed instead of miles or kilometres per hour? Well, it begins with an interesting yet simple story. Seafarers used to toss lengths of knotted rope measuring 47 feet and three inches from their ship to estimate travelling speed. The term 'knot' was derived from this method of measurement, and eventually became the accepted unit of speed for travel at sea and in the air.

The use of nautical miles is also more appropriate for air travel as planes, like ships, traverse vast distances across the globe, which is a sphere. This is because a nautical mile represents one-sixtieth, or a minute of arc, of longitude at the equator. There are therefore 60 nautical miles to one degree. As flying around the Earth at the equator means travelling 360 degrees, circumnavigating the globe means travelling 21,600 (360 multiplied by 60) nautical miles.

WHY DO SOME ROUTES TAKE LONGER TO FLY IN ONE DIRECTION THAN IN THE OTHER?

If you're a frequent traveller, you may notice that on some days, it takes 13-and-a-half hours to fly from Kuala Lumpur to London but only 12-and-a-half hours on the return leg. Why is this so? Very simple indeed! This is due to the strong westerly winds or jet streams, which can be up to 150 knots or more in strength.

During the winter season, there are always headwinds blowing against the plane. It's just like walking against the direction of a travelator at the airport. If you want to go faster, get on the travelator that is going in the same direction you're heading. So when flying to London, one is usually affected by headwinds while on the way back you have the benefit of a tailwind. Hence, planes normally arrive earlier than scheduled from London.

FROM SUBSONIC TO SUPERSONIC

A plane from Kuala Lumpur to Paris would typically cruise at around 30,000 to 38,000 feet depending on passengers and freight carried on board. Passengers have asked me if the aircraft can break the sound barrier if it is aided by a strong tailwind in a jet stream.

The answer is no. Airbus and Boeing planes flying currently are all subsonic planes. This means they are designed to fly below the speed of sound. Even if there is a strong tailwind pushing the plane forward, and ground speed has exceeded the theoretical speed of sound, in reality, the plane has not gone supersonic.

The confusion arises from misunderstanding that arises regarding ground speed and the plane's speed. Ground speed is the speed at which an object travels relative to a fixed point on the Earth's surface. The difference between ground speed and airspeed is caused by the influence of winds on the overall speed of the aircraft.

For example, if you were walking at a speed of 2 mph on a travelator which is also moving at 2 mph, your actual speed as observed by a person not on the moving walkway would be 4 mph. However, as far as you are concerned, you're still walking at 2 mph.

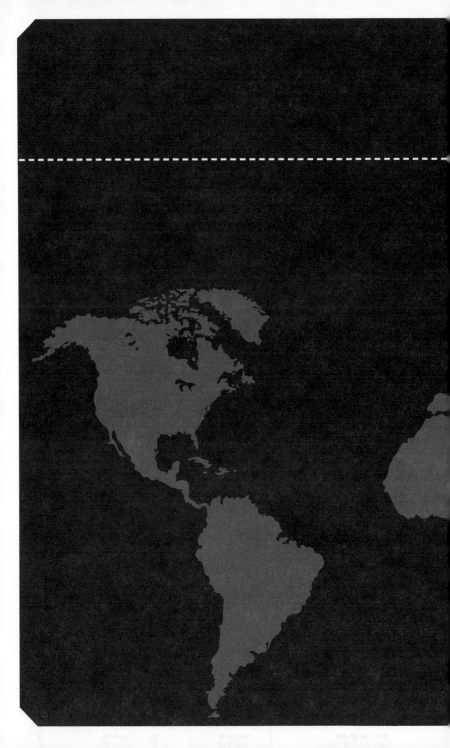

PART III

COMING DOWN TO EARTH:
WHEN IT'S TIME TO LAND

CHAPTER 13

I THOUGHT I SAW AN AIRPORT

When you shouldn't land just yet

You're looking forward to arriving at your destination. The plane lowers its landing gear. Suddenly, there's a roar and the gears are retracted. What's going on? Well, the captain is doing a go-around – he's aborting the landing. Why? There are many reasons, such as a severe wind shear causing the landing approach to be dangerous or the runway being blocked by a crippled plane at the last-minute.

A go-around is a very safe manoeuvre, similar to the take-off procedure. Pilots practise it all the time and are encouraged to do so anytime they feel the landing approach might not be very stable. This practice has averted many potential accidents compared to before, when some pilots tended to push on regardless of the risk, especially when suffering from 'get-home-itis'.

Once, while flying a Boeing 777 from Kuala Lumpur to Perth, my arrival time at Perth happened to clash with the approach of severe thunderstorms and rain, so I reviewed my safety procedures and briefing as usual for the expected difficult landing. Unfortunately, the dark and stormy night also aggravated the situation. I could not land on the runway because of the heavy rain and the situation was made worse by the fact that the runway did not have an Instrument Landing System.

Add to that rough and turbulent wind, I had to abort the landing and divert my plane to Adelaide, about two-and-a-half hours or 1,000 miles away. This decision was made when I found that my minimum fuel level was also fast approaching.

It was the longest diversion that I had ever made. Imagine, a thousand miles is like expecting to arrive in Kuala Lumpur but ending up in Bali instead. When I finally landed at Adelaide instead of Perth, the passengers clapped at the safe touchdown. My senior flight attendant related to me that a passenger had, in fact, commented that it was better to be late than '*dead* on time' after they experienced the severity of that weather at Perth.

One of the most common gripes from passengers is the lack of announcements by pilots. Yes, you should be informed of any unusual manoeuvres, especially in the case of a go-around. This is especially comforting for more fearful flyers. What passengers may not appreciate is that such a manoeuvre is very demanding on the pilots who are, understandably, more concerned with the immediate safety of the plane and its passengers. Give the pilot some time to settle down after performing the manoeuvre and they'll normally come back with the information. Some airlines have responded to this complaint by including a reminder in the go-around checklist to keep passengers informed.

CHAPTER 14

THE BEST AIRPORTS IN THE WORLD
For adrenaline junkies

I've written much about pilot-training and safety drills to allay the concerns of newbie flyers, but some travellers obviously like their rides to be stimulating. 'What are the most exciting, dangerous and unusual airports in the world?' asks a reader of my website.

I've flown around the world to about 80 destinations, and must say the old Hong Kong Kai Tak International Airport was the most exciting and exacting I've come across. Coming in second spot is Tribhuvan Airport in Kathmandu, Nepal; and third, Qamdo Bamda Airport in Tibet, a destination I've yet to visit. All are not just a test of the pilot's mettle; they provide lessons in safety too, as you'll find out.

THE ROOFTOP VIEW: KAI TAK, HONG KONG

The Hong Kong Kai Tak International Airport was quite a challenge to negotiate, to say the least. Firstly, the approach to land on Runway 13 at the airport was very demanding on any pilot in bad weather conditions. Passengers bound for this airport were treated to a pulsating approach during the landing with alarmingly close views of nearby skyscrapers and residential apartments, as the plane banked over to make the final landing.

As a general rule, pilots have the choice of landing from two directions on any single runway, depending on the prevailing wind at the plane's time of arrival.

A plane should, ideally, always land in the direction of the wind. If the wind was blowing from a northwesterly direction, then Runway 31 (so named because the landing direction is around 310 degrees on the compass) at Kai Tak would be used. The opposite approach is known as Runway 13. Due to the high ground on this approach, Runway 13 was far more challenging than Runway 31. Pilots had no alternative but to use this runway if the wind was strong and blowing from a southeasterly direction, or 130 degrees on the compass.

Landing directly in the wind direction was the easy part. What was very tricky was to manoeuvre and turn the plane to line up with the runway in a strong crosswind. Most pilots found landing on Runway 13 a stressful experience, as an auto-landing in foggy weather was not possible due to the unusual turn prior to lining-up.

So, pilots were forced to manually fly the plane at the last-minute with the guidance of a checkerboard located on one of the smaller hills – a visual marking to confirm the approach to Runway 13, on the right.

In 1998, a new airport was built farther west, ending the insightful views of the interiors of offices and apartments of Hong Kongers and their lives. Unfortunately in 1993, before the new airport came into existence, an Air China Boeing 747 was involved in a mishap at Kai Tak. The aircraft had been attempting to land in a gusty and strong crosswind but the adverse weather caused the captain to make an error in judgment – the plane touched down past the two-thirds mark on the runway.

The runway surface was wet from rain and that aggravated the braking efficiency on the remaining one-third of the landing distance. This caused the aircraft to overrun the runway and speed headlong towards a small building that housed the Approach and Landing System for the opposite runway. The captain avoided the impending collision by ground looping (turning around) the plane. Unfortunately, it then headed towards the sea and landed in the water. Even though only partially submerged, the plane was later written off as a total hull loss. Luckily, the accident resulted in only minor injuries to 22 passengers.

WHY LAND IN ADVERSE WEATHER?

Sometimes, pilots are reluctant to abort the landing for fear of being chastised by the management (unlikely today) or inconveniencing the passengers. This, however, can sometimes lead to serious consequences.

I remember some years back, I aborted a landing on a Boeing 777 due to bad weather on the approach to Perth International Airport in Australia and diverted instead to Adelaide, about two hours flight time away. It was costly to the company and it definitely inconvenienced the passengers.

SKIMMING MOUNTAIN TOPS: TRIBHUVAN, KATHMANDU, NEPAL

Getting to Tribhuvan Airport in Kathmandu is like trying to land inside a large bowl. This airport sits in the middle of a valley with mountainous terrain on all sides. Two airlines, one from Thailand and another from Pakistan, have lost a plane each there to the surrounding mountains.

On July 31, 1992, a Thai Airways Airbus A310 from Bangkok crashed into a steep rock face in a remote mountainous area at an altitude of 11,500 feet while trying to make an approach to land at the airport. Investigators found that the accident was likely caused by the captain and controller's bewilderment over language as well as technical problems. This was further aggravated by the airline's failure to provide simulator training to its pilots for the complex Kathmandu approach.

On September 28, 1992, a Pakistan International Airlines Airbus A300 from Karachi also crashed on its approach to the airport. The authorities found that the pilot had descended prematurely at 1,000 feet below the correct flight path. The plane failed to clear the 'tip of the bowl' and crashed into the southern slope. Since then, all pilots who operate into this destination are thoroughly trained to ensure that they're very familiar with the surrounding terrain before being allowed to fly into Kathmandu.

Among the difficulties at this airport: engine failure during take-off, which would require both pilots to work very closely with each other. Turns would be restricted to within four miles, speed has to be at its optimum climbing-rate and the pilot must spiral the plane to the top of the 'bowl' until a safe height is reached, before setting course for home.

To land, pilots have to 'skip' over the edge of the 'bowl', then carry out a steep descent before easing off the dive in order to land the plane safely. An Instrument Landing System could not be properly installed for this airport due to the nature of the terrain, making landing at Kathmandu a task of skilful manoeuvring and very thorough briefings.

IN THIN AIR: QAMDO BAMDA, TIBET

Not just another airport in the mountains that presents unique challenges – located at an elevation of 14,219 feet, it is the world's highest airport and also has the world's longest commercial runway. What is amazing about Qamdo Bamda is that it's located well above the safety level a plane is meant to descend in the event of loss of cabin pressurisation. One of the regulatory requirements for aircraft manufacturers is for the cabin to be pressurised if a plane will be flown more than 10,000 feet above sea level, where the air is considered too thin to support a safe level of oxygen supply. This is to protect the crew and passengers from the risk of lack of oxygen. Even prolonged exposure to the air at 10,000 feet can result in sluggish thinking and dimmed vision.

Generally, most passengers can tolerate this altitude, where there's about 25 per cent less oxygen than there is at sea level. So you can imagine how some would feel upon arrival at Qamdo. Some will experience dizziness and breathing difficulties; inbound passengers are warned to move slowly when disembarking from the plane.

The thin air also affects the performance of the plane. The low air-density means more power is needed for lift-off, hence the record-breaking length of the runway – 18,045 feet. Only Air China and China Southern Airlines currently fly to this destination.

The old Kai Tak International Airport in Hong Kong is history. It's been replaced by shiny new Chek Lap Kok, which has been ranked one of the best airports in the world. Getting into Hong Kong has been a breeze for pilots since 1998, although it may be a bit less exciting now.

That said, when things are safe, they're rarely exciting. And when you're flying towards a difficult landing strip, the last thing you want is an 'exciting' experience! Safety is absolutely paramount and pilots strive to maintain the highest standards at all times and in all conditions. I hope most of your flights are not boring, but rest assured that your pilots are always doing their utmost to make your journey as safe as possible.

CHAPTER 15

BEING DITCHED
Learning to crash well

There's more water than land mass on this planet, so flight and cabin crew train very hard to ensure we know what to do in the unfortunate event of a crash into water. One of the most common questions put to me by fearful travellers is what happens if a plane crashes into the sea.

Although the chances of this occurring are extremely low – about one in eight million – it could happen. In January 2009, a US Airways Airbus A320 crashed into the frigid Hudson River after birds knocked out both engines. Miraculously, all 155 passengers and crew on board survived.

To explain what happens when an aircraft crashes into the sea, I first need to elaborate more on ditching, a term we use to refer to a landing on water, be it controlled or not.

Controlled ditching can arise when the airplane is forced to land in the sea because it's about to run out of fuel (engines still running at this stage), perhaps due to fuel leakage. Uncontrolled ditching arises when the airplane has no more power left to manoeuvre the plane for a touchdown onto the water.

HOW TO SURVIVE BEING DITCHED

Unlike the Titanic, which notoriously carried far too few lifeboats to accommodate all its passengers, a Boeing 777, for example, has eight slide rafts, each capable of carrying an average of 58 passengers or a total capacity of 466 survivors. This is far greater than the total number of passengers a Boeing 777 can carry.

Assuming that a safe ditching has taken place over the sea, the 58 survivors in each slide raft would have some equipment and survival paraphernalia on board to keep them busy until rescue arrives.

Out of the eight slide rafts, two are equipped with emergency locator transmitters (ELT) that are activated automatically when they hit water. The ELT assists rescue aircraft in pinpointing the position of survivors floating in the sea. It can transmit emergency signals for up to 50 hours at a range of 100 to 280 miles.

An orange fabric canopy can be erected over the slide raft to protect against the sun's rays. The survival bag within each life raft also has many aids to attract the attention of rescue aircraft or ships. One such item is the heliograph – a specially designed mirror used to reflect beams of sunlight at rescuers.

Then there are the night flares to be used when a rescue aircraft or ship is sighted. To make the location of the raft more visible in daylight hours, sea dye markers are provided to ensure an obvious trail is visible. Each individual life vest is also attached with a whistle for attracting attention.

If survivors are thirsty, there is drinking water on board. Hungry? There is barley glucose sugar to munch on. Feeling seasick? There are Sea Legs tablets from the First Aid kit. When it gets dark, there are flashlights. If the raft leaks, it can be mended with repair clamps; excess water can be sponged and even a bailing bucket is provided. There is also a hand-pump to top up a slightly deflated raft. Feeling bored? There's a survival manual to read too. Unlike the days of the Titanic, modern search and rescue teams are also better equipped to provide faster and more efficient aid when an SOS is sent.

How long can a plane stay afloat after a successful ditching? It depends on how well the ditching was executed. A perfect landing will enable the plane to stay afloat like a boat for quite a while. But a badly executed one can have tragic consequences. Let's get to the bottom of this scenario so that, as aircraft passengers, you will be truly educated on the procedures in the event of a ditching.

SOME REAL LIFE CASES OF BEING DITCHED

The survival rate for this procedure is actually very high. Ditching, however, is distinct from water crashes – ditching is intentional while water crashes usually involve an uncontrolled aircraft hitting the water at extremely high speeds. Ditching survival rates depend on the size of the aircraft, the condition of the water surface and the speed at which the pilot eases the plane onto the water.

On January 15, 2009, Flight 1549 operated by US Airways ditched into the Hudson River in New York after suffering multiple bird-strikes. In this incident, the pilot, Captain Chesley Sullenberger – more popularly known as Sully – made a perfect water landing, saving the lives of all 155 passengers and crew. The Airbus A320 he was flying was able to stay afloat because the plane was not damaged above the waterline. However, below the floating wing, there was slight damage to the cargo compartment; the left engine was detached and sank about 65 feet into the river.

Most commercial airliners are designed to float for a reasonable length of time, enabling passengers and crew to exit safely. The evacuation slides around the exit doors are designed to double up as flotation devices and life rafts.

When Flight 1549 landed on water, it remained on the surface for quite some time before slowly sinking as it drifted downriver. The cabin of the plane is designed to act like the hull of a boat and will stay afloat as long as there are no leaks. Unfortunately, the impact with the water had ripped open a hole on the underside of the airplane and twisted the fuselage, causing the cargo door to pop open, slowly filling the plane with water from the rear.

Pilots are also able to shut off all intake and outlet valves on the entire plane by activating a ditching switch, making the cabin fully watertight. This would easily allow the plane to stay afloat for more than an hour. However, in the Hudson River case, damage to the cargo compartment impaired buoyancy.

Nevertheless, the plane stayed afloat long enough for everyone to get out safely. Fortunately, there was a small armada of police boats, fireboats, tugboats and the Coast Guard to help rescue the passengers. Some of the boats were even seen supporting the jetliner on its side to keep it afloat for longer.

DON'T HIT THE BIRDS

Bird-strike is a risk that is potentially disastrous for any airplane taking off. The pilot's skill in handling such a strike that results in engine failures is the last bastion against such a disaster.

Captain Sully had perfectly performed such an incredible task. He saved the lives of all onboard his Airbus A320.

Boeing 777 engines can withstand bird-strikes well because all modern jet engines are subjected to the 'chicken gun test' before certification. This 'test' by the FAA stipulates that planes must be able to withstand a strike from at least an 8-pound bird.

As such, large passenger jets can safely withstand being hit by at least a four-pound bird but problems can arise with flocks of birds. Planes are often struck by flying birds but these aren't frequently reported because planes are designed to take such impact. It becomes dangerous only if a large bird strikes at a critical moment. Experts have calculated that a 12-pound goose hitting an aircraft during liftoff would generate a force equivalent to a 1,000-pound object being dropped from a height of 10 feet!

Many have asked how Flight 1549 was able to glide despite the damage? To answer that, it is good to first note that most planes are designed to glide with the engines switched off. The success of the glide depends on the altitude of the planes – the higher the better. At 40,000 feet, a plane can glide 100 nautical miles with all engines switched off. Unfortunately, the US Airways flight was in the worst situation when the engines were completely lost at around 3,000 feet, where a successful glide would be quite difficult.

The National Transportation Safety Board (NTSB) ran a series of tests using Airbus simulators in France to see if Flight 1549 could have returned safely to LaGuardia Airport. The simulation started immediately following the bird-strike and, knowing in advance that they were going to suffer a bird-strike and that the engines couldn't be restarted, four out of four pilots were able to turn the A320 back to LaGuardia and land on Runway 13.

When the NTSB later imposed a 30-second delay before the pilots could respond – recognising that it wasn't reasonable to expect a pilot to assess the situation and react instantly – all four pilots crashed.

This proved that Captain Sully had made the best decision to ditch the plane in the Hudson. The question of how long a plane stays afloat after a successful water landing depends on the skill of the pilot.

As with everything in life, human skill and experience will always be needed as tools to be used in dire circumstances. Captain Scully saved the day – and many lives – when he chose to ditch the A320. It wasn't just down to the capability of the aircraft to stay afloat until everyone could be evacuated. It was also because he was an amazingly skilful pilot who knew exactly what to do and how to manoeuvre the aircraft onto water.

ALSO DITCHED SUCCESSFULLY

Besides Flight 1549, there have been at least three other successful ditchings in recent decades.

In January 2002, a Garuda Indonesia Boeing 737 safely ditched onto a river near Yogyakarta after experiencing a twin engine failure during heavy rain. The pilots tried to restart the engines several times before making the decision to land the aircraft in the water.

In 1963, a Tupolev 124 operated by Aeroflot ditched onto a river as it ran out of fuel. The aircraft floated and was towed ashore by a tugboat, which it had nearly hit as it came down on the water. All 52 passengers onboard escaped without injuries.

In 1956, a Pan Am flight ditched into the Pacific Ocean after losing two of its four engines. All 31 on board survived.

Paying close attention to the safety procedures explained by the flight attendants will go a long way towards saving lives, in the event of such an emergency.

CHAPTER 16

THE SOUND OF ONE ENGINE FLYING
Or none: when engines fail

Is a two-engine plane flying with one engine similar to a bird flying with one wing? No, because technology is now advanced enough that a twin-engine plane with one functioning engine can fly as well as with one with two engines, albeit with a few limitations.

Today, twin-engine planes that fly over long stretches of water must abide by stringent requirements under the Extended Twin-Engine Operational Performance Standards (ETOPS) regulations – some people humorously think it should stand for 'Engines Turn or Passengers Swim'!

Many newer twin-engine wide body planes, especially the Boeing 777, 787 and Airbus A330, fly across the Pacific and Atlantic Ocean. All are ETOPS-certified, meaning that they are capable of flying beyond an hour from a suitable airport in the event of an emergency with the remaining engine. Flying overland is not a problem but, over oceans, this could be an issue if the aircraft aren't certified. To permit long-distance flights with twin-engine aircraft, rigorous rules have been set.

Firstly, aircraft must be built and designed with proven engines. The performances of the planes are monitored by the manufacturers and authorities. They must demonstrate a high level of reliability and the aircraft must have redundancies to ensure all systems continue to function when an engine fails in flight.

Once all these are in place, the airlines have to be certified and assessed before their planes are given the ETOPS certification. This allows twin-engine planes to fly on one engine for as long as 90, 120 or 180 minutes (up to 330 minutes on the latest Boeing 777) over water.

The record is held by a United Airlines Boeing 777 that flew for three hours and 12 minutes on one engine on a flight from Auckland to San Francisco. The captain had to shut down one engine due to a mechanical problem and landed safely at Kona International Airport in Hawaii.

Three- and four-engine aircraft don't require ETOPS certification as their reliability is inherently adequate for dealing with any engine failure. That said, some are of the view that two-engine ETOPS planes have an even higher level of safety than three- or four-engine planes when it comes to redundancy and reliability.

So which is safer, two- or four-engines planes? They're equally safe. Aircraft engines are very reliable today (barring any large bird-strikes on the engines) and there's hardly any risk that passengers will have to swim to shore.

AND IF YOU LOSE BOTH ENGINES...

Now, to answer the big question: Can a two-engine plane still fly and land safely after losing both engines? This is a question that is frequently asked and needs to be answered to dispel any doubt.

A 'dead-stick landing' is when all the engines of a plane are lost and the pilot is forced to land on any flat open ground. The term was coined long ago – the 'stick' refers to the wooden propellers on old planes and not the flight controls as many may assume. The controls on most planes can still function even without engine power. Hence, the plane is still controllable in such situations.

This reminds me of when I won the dead-stick spot landing competition at the Royal Selangor Flying Club many years back. In this competition, pilots flying single-engine planes were asked to touch down nearest to the threshold (beginning) of the runway. If a pilot landed short, he would be disqualified. Those were the good old days when flying was cheaper – petrol was less than US$30 per barrel – and pilots could hone their skills while having loads of fun flying.

Dead-stick landing comes in handy in the event of a glide landing. This was precisely what happened to a Canadian pilot in 1983. He managed to glide-land a Boeing 767 safely on a disused runway when it ran out of fuel due to an error in the refuelling process – given 22,000 pounds of fuel instead of 22,000 kilograms!

In my 45 years of flying, I've practised for and been tested many times on how to cope with the failure or either one or two engines on a four-engine plane. However, I've never had the misfortune of encountering such incidents in real life. Safety experts say that the odds of an engine failing is about one in 800,000 while the odds of a two-engine failure are even more remote – one in eight million. In fact, you'd have a better chance of winning the lottery!

The airline industry continues to promote engine-failure training and takes no chances in its efforts to ensure the safety of air travellers. When I attended the pilot-selection process, one of the ways to check our flying potential was to test our psychomotor skills using an archaic mechanical bench. Fast-forward to the present and pilot-selection is more advanced and stringent. Selection is done using the ADAPT system, a computerised selection and assessment process that's also used to pick F1 drivers, ensuring that new pilots are even more adept in their skills.

Regardless of how remote the chances are of a dead-stick emergency becoming reality, pilots are still subjected to many, many rigorous check flights so that they will always be prepared for engine failure during all takeoffs. It's something that is ingrained into the pilots' consciousness, so they know instinctively what needs to be done should such an event ever occur.

HOW TO HANDLE A DEAD-STICK LANDING

Unlike a normal powered landing, a dead-stick landing requires skill and good judgment. An error in selecting the flaps or landing gear prior to touchdown is generally irrecoverable and the plane will land short of the runway.

A plane with two failed engines will glide a distance of around 100 nautical miles from 40,000 feet. For the more technically minded readers, let me elaborate a little on this glide landing technique. From my experience on an Airbus A330 simulator, the pilot should position the plane on the centreline of a runway at a height of about 6,000 feet when 15 nautical miles out at 170 knots and Flaps 1. When assured of a safe touchdown, the pilot should lower the landing gear at around 1,500 to 800 feet to be assured of safe touch down on the runway.

However, on a twin-engine Airbus, when both the engines are lost, only limited electrical power is available with the aid of the ram air turbine (RAT), an emergency generator that automatically kicks in when it senses two engine failures. The RAT has a mini-fan and is powered by airflow as the plane glides down for a landing.

To lower the landing gear in this scenario, the system makes use of gravity. This is achieved by releasing a mechanical lock. To stop the plane, it has the emergency brake (accumulator brake pressure) to supply about seven applications – enough to bring the plane to a complete stop.

YES, WE CAN

There have been several instances of commercial planes successfully carrying out dead-stick landings.

In July 1983, an Air Canada Boeing 767 ran out of fuel en-route from Montreal to Edmonton. However, the crew managed to make a successful dead-stick landing at an abandoned airfield at Gimli where a car rally was in progress.

In August 2001, an Airbus A330 near the Azores in the Atlantic Ocean lost both engines as a result of fuel starvation. The crew was able to glide the plane for 20 minutes – or about 115 miles – to an airfield, averting a water landing. None of the 13 crew members or 293 passengers was seriously injured.

In January 2009, a US Airways Airbus A320 made successful dead-stick water landing on the Hudson River in New York with no loss of lives amongst the 155 people on board.

A dead-stick landing is often quite challenging. Recently, at the end of the training course for my two hardworking Japanese students, both requested that I set up a scenario in the flight simulator to enable them to practise the exercise. I'm happy to report that both successfully landed the plane without any problems. It gave them tremendous confidence knowing they may do just as well as Captain Sully of the Hudson River water landing fame!

IT'S RISKY GOING THE SUPERMARKET TOO

All airliners have the capability to glide when all engines are lost. They will not plummet like a stone but will continue to glide horizontally while descending. The success rate of this very rare incident shows that not all is lost even when a plane loses all propulsive power in flight.

Lest the thought of engine failure worries you, let me reassure you that airplane engines are generally very reliable and flying is one of the safest forms of travel. It is safer than you going to the supermarket in your car. A US National Safety Council study showed that flying is many times safer than travelling by car and that the people who died on the road during a six-month period was equal to all the commercial air travel fatalities worldwide of the last 40 years combined.

Here's another amusing story from an air traveller who blogged about her scary experience on board an Airbus A320 flight.

THE PLANE'S ENGINE DIED. S-T-O-P-P-E D!

As the aircraft was being pushed out of the aerobridge prior to starting the engines, its auxiliary power unit (APU) malfunctioned, causing a blackout in the cabin, leaving only essential lightings on.

The passenger thought that the engines had shut down. She promptly kicked up a big fuss and broadcast this on her blog much later. Here's an excerpt from her blog:

> All of a sudden, the plane's engine DIED. S-T-O-P-P-E D. All the lights went off; no sound was heard from the engine or any equipment in the plane whatsoever. It was total silence from the plane and all we heard were whispers of confusion from (sic) our part.
>
> Fearing for our safety as images of the engine dying again flashed in our minds, we informed the crew on board we are (sic) getting off! After all, the plane was not 100 per cent fit to fly and it should be checked

under any circumstances. What if the engine dies again while taking off? What if during mid-air or, during landing?

The passenger had mistakenly thought the engines had failed when in fact, it was only the APU that had malfunctioned. The engines hadn't even been started yet. It was just a consequential electrical malfunction.

This is a case of a little knowledge being a dangerous thing, especially since the writer had incorrectly deduced that the engines were not safe to continue the flight with and broadcast this distorted picture to all at large on her blog.

It's fine for someone to air their grievances online, but I believe it isn't proper to blow things out of proportion. Such scaremongering does not serve any purpose except to create more fear among passengers who are already worried about other flight hazards. Unnecessary alarm too could have been kept at bay if the pilot had explained the problem at hand.

Where airplanes are concerned, there are many devices in place to ensure malfunctions are addressed by other standby or backup systems. In this case, batteries were available for the standby services when the APU failure occurred.

CHAPTER 17

CAN I JUMP NOW?

Parachutes for passengers and airplanes

Ian, a young flyer from Scotland wrote to me with many questions because of his scary experiences when he first started flying. On one of his flights to London's Heathrow airport, he experienced severe turbulence accompanied by a loud bang. The plane seemed to drop and he thought he was going to die. The rough ride stopped after two minutes; the aircraft stabilised. Then, without warning, it seemed to drop again. Ian turned around and saw the other passengers holding onto their seats. Some were screaming. There had been an announcement, warning passengers of the turbulence but Ian had no idea it would be that bad. Thankfully, the plane landed without incident. Here's one very interesting question that Ian asked: Why are planes not equipped with parachutes so passengers can jump out in the event of a crash landing?

NO, NOT YET

First of all, equipping every passenger with a parachute on commercial planes is not very practical and fraught with difficulty. Very simply, commercial planes are not designed for easy exits at high altitudes and speeds. For starters, the doors cannot be opened in mid-air unless the plane is depressurised below 10,000 feet.

Even if it were possible to jump out of the plane strapped to a parachute, due to the high speed and turbulent air flow, any passenger who attempts this would get hurt during the exit, including hitting the plane or getting sucked into the engines!

Nor is it easy to operate a parachute and land safely without basic training. The temperature at 40,000 feet is extremely cold, about −56 degrees Celsius. The lack of oxygen at such altitudes may also cause the jumper to fall unconscious very quickly.

HOW ABOUT NOW?

Most of the time, one wouldn't know if the plane is definitely going to crash. By the time a crash is imminent, passengers will not have time for parachutes anyway. Due to this huge uncertainty, who would decide on the right time for passengers to strap on their parachutes and commence an orderly jump out of the plane? If there is an emergency, the captain's main responsibility is to immediately solve the problem and attempt a safe landing. He simply would have no time for any other matters.

There have been three occasions where planes have successfully crash landed.

In 1983, an Air Canada Boeing 767 ran out of fuel and landed safely on a disused runway where go-kart races were being held. All on board survived.

In 2001, a chartered Transat Air A330 made a forced-landing at an Atlantic Ocean island when both its engines failed because of a fuel leak, saving 306 lives in this longest ever glide-landing of a commercial airliner.

In 2009, a US Airways Airbus A320 ditched into the Hudson River in New York. The plane had to make a controlled water-landing onto the river after losing thrust in both engines due to a bird-strike at about 3,000 feet. This happened just three minutes into the flight after a normal take-off from LaGuardia. Miraculously, all 155 passengers and crew survived. Within those three minutes, it would not have been possible for all onboard to jump out in time, even if there were parachutes available.

Most aircraft accidents occur either immediately after take-off or just before landing. There is usually no time, like in the case of the Hudson River ditching, to get all passengers, including the old and young, to put on their parachutes in orderly fashion. It would also be an exercise in futility as very few have ever experienced sky-diving with parachutes. Additionally, for the parachute to open safely there must be sufficient altitude for it to deploy.

NOW?

Another problem is the exit speed of the jumper. A commercial airplane cruises at 400 to 500 knots. Standard parachutes are made to open at speeds around 110 knots. Jumping out at such high speeds would rip the fabric of the canopy to shreds unless the plane is flying at a much slower speed.

As the sharp Irish playwright, George Bernard Shaw, said: 'The optimist invented the airplane, the pessimist, the parachute.' Statistics allow me to say with confidence that you're much safer flying on a plane than travelling in a car.

WHY NOT A PARACHUTE FOR THE WHOLE PLANE?

Why not, indeed. Can large parachutes be used to save planes from falling from the sky during an emergency? Here's an e-mail from a curious reader of my website:

> I am a frequent flyer on long and short-haul flights. I admit I have never been totally relaxed throughout the flight, regardless of how smooth it was. I have also been concerned about issues that may occur during flying.

I have a question which may sound silly: Is there any research being made to develop mega-parachutes that can be attached to a plane like huge balloons that will allow the aircraft to land in case of total engine failure?

CAPS FOR SMALL PLANES

Interestingly, the concept of fitting parachutes on planes has so far been fairly successful in small planes only. The device is known as the Cirrus Airframe Parachute System (CAPS). When a plane's engine quits mid-flight, all the pilot has to do is pull a red, T-shaped handle in the cockpit and the parachute will deploy within seconds. This will help bring the aircraft safely to the ground. The force of impact when using the system is similar to that experienced when falling from a height of about 10 feet only.

The first successful deployment of CAPS was in Texas in 2002, when it helped a pilot who had difficulty controlling his plane land safely. It was the first emergency application of an airframe parachute on a certified aircraft in aviation history. The system, however, encountered a major setback months later when the manufacturer of CAPS was sued by two families over the failure of the parachute to deploy in another air crash.

JUMPING TOGETHER OFF BIG PLANES

Despite the shortcomings highlighted above, research has already been carried out into developing a similar system for big commercial airliners. At first glance, it does seem a little impractical to implement this idea but after one Air France Airbus A330 crash that saw the plane dropping at around 10,000 feet per minute from 38,000 feet, it appears the time is ripe for the aviation industry to take a serious look at what once seemed like a preposterous idea.

To implement this, the biggest challenge is to develop a parachute strong enough to be used on bigger, faster planes. NASA has been using such parachutes for spacecraft for decades, but space capsules cater only for a few astronauts while commercial aircraft have hundreds of passengers.

The most technologically advanced parachute at present can carry up to about 4,000 pounds in weight only, while the CAPS currently being used only works on small planes weighing half that with a cruise speed of 175 mph. In comparison, the Boeing 787 and Airbus A380 weigh anything from half to over a million pounds. As such, aviation experts question whether parachutes can ever be attached to such planes as their great weight and high cruise speed would make such equipment impractical.

Some have suggested that rather than having one large parachute, the plane be divided into smaller sections with airframe parachutes for each. Such an aircraft would have a body with a few capsules located between the cockpit and tail. Each capsule would house a passenger seating area and could detach itself from the fuselage during an emergency.

A GOOD IDEA IN SEARCH OF A SOLUTION

The idea of having a parachute for planes may seem fanciful as well as cost-prohibitive but the system could, one day, save the lives of hundreds of passengers and crew when it is finally perfected.

In 2009, Air France Flight 447 from Rio de Janeiro to Paris was trapped in a severe thunderstorm. Apparently, this happened because the radar setting was improperly tilted, resulting in the inability to spot intense weather activity ahead of the plane. As a result, the aircraft's pitot tubes became iced up and blocked, resulting in unreliable airspeed readings. This led the plane into a stall, a problem compounded by the relief pilot's mishandling of the stall recovery process.

The captain, who was resting at the back of the plane, was urgently recalled to the cockpit to help, but it was too late – Flight 447 crashed into the Atlantic, killing all 228 people onboard. Had a parachute system been in place, perhaps the tragedy could have been avoided.

PART IV

INTERLUDE: HUMAN AFFAIRS

CHAPTER 18

IT'S GETTING CROWDED UP THERE
Congested skies and humans behaving badly

I've encountered a few interesting instances of air rage in my flying career. Experts say that such behaviour likely stems the general stress of air travel, likely made worse by delays. Air rage can be aggravated when alcohol is introduced into the bloodstream, perhaps in an ironic attempt to handle the stress. It can lead to unpredictable behaviour at high altitude.

An example of this happened on the way to Europe. A flight attendant had reported to me that a drunken passenger had repeatedly flashed her when no one was looking. Despite several warnings, he persisted with his lewd behaviour. He was duly escorted off the plane by the security officials in Frankfurt and fined where it hurt.

From reports, incidents of air rage or the propensity of passengers to lose their cool has increased considerably in recent years. This may be attributed to air travel being more affordable than ever.

Some passengers don't realise that they cannot behave on a plane as they would on the ground. Even simple prohibitions against smoking and the use of mobiles are sometimes disregarded, as these are not considered offences on land.

LOOSE LIPS SINK SHIPS

This saying was part of the Allied forces propaganda campaign during the second world war to prevent Nazi U-Boats from knowing about and sinking Allied shipping lines. It still applies: to passengers who can't seem to stop using their mobiles on flying vessels. Once, while waiting for passengers to board one of my flights, I observed that the duty manager was having difficulty stopping a passenger from using his mobile phone before boarding. It appears that many air travellers take this ban very lightly.

'Is the fly-by-wire system really so sensitive that micro signals from mobile phones affect it?' a frequent air traveller once asked me. He lives in the Middle East and noticed that some of the locals on his flights used their mobiles non-stop, and no planes had crashed – yet.

Let me explain a bit about the various types of portable electronic devices. The Federal Aviation Administration

Regulations have classified such devices into two groups, namely A and B.

Those in Group A are more critical as they intentionally radiate or transmit strong radio signals and are not allowed to be used onboard the airplane at any time. These items include mobile phones, pagers, walkie-talkies, transmitters that remotely control devices like toys, citizen band radios, amateur radio transceivers and battery-powered calculators with printers.

Devices that fall under Group B are those that do not intentionally radiate and transmit radio signals but nevertheless emit low powered 'electronic noise'. These may not be switched on during the taxiing, take-off, approach and landing phases but you can use them once the seatbelt sign is off at above 10,000 feet and during the cruise. Examples include laptop computers, video recorders, audio and playback devices, MP3 and DVD players, electronic entertainment devices, electric shavers, calculators and FM or TV receivers.

HAYWIRELESS MAYHEM

Prohibited devices can cause airplanes to do unguided turns during the approach to land, navigational systems to go haywire, fuel quantity to read zero and confuse onboard computers. Many pilots have also reported interference to their communications and navigation equipment during the various stages of flight – it's important to not surreptitiously use your mobile phone in the air.

Ever noticed how, when you place your mobile phone beside the car radio or laptop speakers, you can hear a squelchy noise when someone calls you? That is someone's mobile phone injecting a current into the wiring of your electronic equipment. This electronic interference is undesirable, especially when a plane is approaching for an auto-landing that relies a lot on the various electronic signals to keep the plane locked onto the centre beam of the runway.

Generally, if an unusual electronic fault is detected, an internal warning system normally alerts the pilot. If he's unable to find or troubleshoot the fault in the usual manner, the next step is to find out from the flight attendants whether any of the passengers are using a prohibited electronic device. Very often, when the offending device is found and switched off the navigation system returns to normal.

In 2002, pilots of a Boeing 737 making a landing approach at Chicago Midway Airport noticed an erroneous airplane position from the course deviation indicator. At one point, it showed that the plane was on course but the next moment, off-course and too far south. When they finally sighted the runway, they were too high and too far north to land. The pilots eventually discovered that a passenger was using her mobile phone. When the device was turned off, the cockpit instruments returned to normal and the Boeing 737 landed safely.

Of course, this incident did not necessarily mean a crisis was at hand. But while electronic interference alone might not be a major threat, combined with other factors like bad weather and pilot fatigue, these minor incidents could contribute to major accidents. So please maintain radio silence with your mobiles on all flights.

CHAPTER 19

HEY, BABES

How about a lifetime of free air travel?

Let's talk about the birds, bees and special deliveries. The expectant mother somehow avoided detection of her late-stage pregnancy during check-in boarded my flight. Alas (for her) she was quickly discovered by a crew member who was aware of flight regulations regarding heavily pregnant women. She immediately consulted me on what to do. It was the captain's duty to handle the situation...

Airline policy regarding carriage for pregnant women can be summarised as follows:

If the pregnancy is below 28 weeks, the expectant mother is allowed to fly but will need to sign a release and indemnity certificate to absolve the airline of any liabilities should anything unforeseen happen.

If the pregnancy is 28 to 34 weeks along, the expectant mother will need to obtain a medical certificate valid for at least one week from her doctor stating the expected due date and her fitness to fly. She will also need to sign the release and indemnity certificate.

Any woman whose pregnancy is beyond 35 weeks will not be allowed to fly.

I applied the rules. The expectant lady on my flight did not satisfy the second condition and was politely told to disembark. The captain would otherwise be held accountable should anything happen. I felt sorry for the crying mother who was very reluctant to leave. It was probably not her fault as she may not have been properly informed about the regulations.

IS IT SAFE FOR PREGNANT WOMEN TO FLY ON A NON-PRESSURISED FLIGHT?
This popped up in my Inbox:

Dear Captain Lim, my husband and I booked a trip to the Bahamas six months ago. Then I got pregnant and I am five months along right now. I know it's relatively safe to fly on a commercial pressurised airplane; however, there is a 30-minute flight between

Florida and the island which, I imagine, will be in a non-pressurised airplane. Do you think it's safe for me to take this flight?

I told her the general rule for the carriage of an expectant mother is that no medical certificate is required unless her pregnancy is between week 28 and 34. As such, she should be able to fly without having to produce a medical certificate. Airlines are generally more concerned about the possibility of pregnant passengers giving birth during the flight.

Additionally, if she had recently experienced heavy bleeding, threatened miscarriage or high blood pressure, she would have been advised to consult a doctor prior to the flight.

It's true that many doctors have advised expectant mothers to avoid flying at high altitudes in non-pressurised aircraft. This is to minimise the possibility of miscarriage due to insufficient oxygen reaching the foetus. However, if her flight is around 5,000 to 8,000 feet for the duration of 30 minutes, I believe it should not be a problem. Having said that, she should obtain expert medical advice if she would like to travel.

IT'S A GIRL! A CITIZEN OF THE WORLD...
Congratulations! Assuming that all the conditions of carriage of expectant mothers are satisfied but the unexpected happens

and a child is born during the flight, what's the baby's place of birth and citizenship?

Try to follow what I'm about to tell you carefully. There was a passenger who gave birth onboard a British Airways jet flying from London to Boston. The pilot received permission to land in Nova Scotia, Canada, due to the unexpected delivery but the baby had been born before the plane could land.

When it came to filling out the birth certificate, figuring out the child's citizenship and place of birth was a complicated affair. The mother was an Egyptian woman with an American passport on a plane that took off from Britain, bound for the US, but landed in Canada. Here, for customs purposes, the baby was considered a Canadian citizen because she was born over Canadian airspace.

The United Nations considers a child born inflight to have been born in the plane's registered country. However, some countries point to the city where the child first disembarked the plane as the place of birth and to the airplane's registered country as the place of citizenship. There's no consensus. In most cases, the baby initially assumes the nationality of the mother for immediate arrival formalities.

According to British Airways, which prohibits women from travelling in the last month of pregnancy, in-air births are rare. But they do happen at a rate of about one delivery per year onboard its flights. Most flight attendants are trained in birthing procedure in case one of their pregnant passengers can't wait until the plane lands.

DOES A BABY BORN INFLIGHT GET FREE AIR TRAVEL FOR LIFE?

And now, the answer to the million-dollar question. The unwritten rule is whispered like this: the reason airlines impose restrictions on expectant mothers is so they never have to provide a lifetime worth of free tickets to a baby born onboard their planes.

If you're now planning your trip to coincide with your baby's very own touchdown on planet Earth, it's not going to happen... with three exceptions: Baby Dararasami Thongchareon arrived two months ahead of schedule on a Thai Airways Boeing 747 flight, baby Mohd Aliff Mohd Faud was born on Asia Pacific Airlines flight and another baby, on board an AirAsia Airbus A320. All three were granted these privileges – because their births had special significance of luck and good fortune for the carriers in their respective cultures.

So, dear reader, if you're expecting and the delivery date is coming up, please get clearance from your doctor before flying. If you can delay your flight to a later date, then please do so. The priority here is to ensure the safety of yourself and your precious 'cargo'. Nothing else is as important.

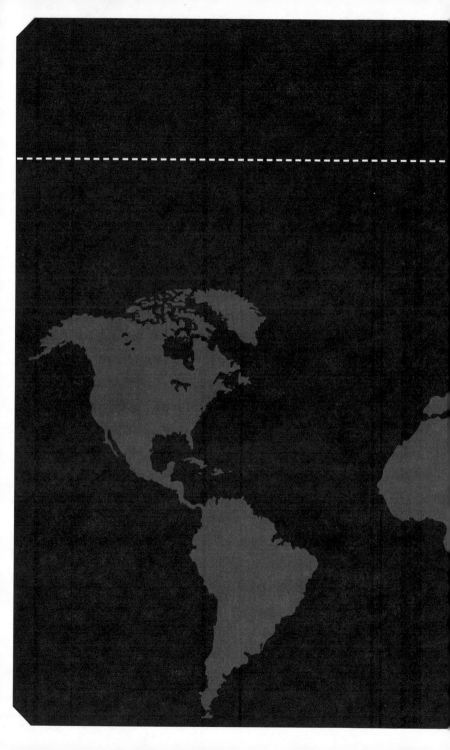

PART V

A BIT ON THE AIRLINE BUSINESS
AND THEIR FLYING MACHINES

CHAPTER 20

THE STUFF AIRLINES ARE REALLY MADE OF
Fuel for thought

First, some trivia before the serious talk. The scene – a gas station in New Jersey, USA, in December 2012. A fuel truck has, apparently, mistakenly delivered jet fuel to it instead of normal gasoline.

Here's a question all petrolheads want answered: Will pumping jet fuel into your car make it fast and furious? Well, no, it won't. Unless you drive a diesel car, putting jet fuel into your tank will likely result in a stalled engine. That's what happened to several drivers when they refuelled at that gas station in New Jersey that day.

The truth is, jet fuel is basically kerosene, which is closer to regular old diesel fuel. You'd only be able to run it in a diesel car, although it won't lubricate the fuel system as normal diesel fuel would.

On the other hand, smaller flying club piston-engined planes such as the Cessna 172 use aviation gas or avgas that normally has a very high octane rating (often around 100). You can use avgas for your car, but it has only one small advantage – helping to stop premature detonation, or engine-knocking. However, this would still require modifications to the carburettor or injector settings.

Just thought I'd clear that up. Now I'll tell you all about the stuff that airlines are really made of.

WHY THE CONCORDE IS NO MORE

Airplanes consume much fuel, which is one of the reasons the supersonic Concorde was a commercial failure. An airline's survival, just like any other business, depends on making profit. But with fuel prices escalating, many legacy airlines are on the verge of bankruptcy or have been forced to merge in order to stay commercially viable. Low-cost carriers find it easier to thrive because of their operating philosophy.

Airplane fuel is seldom measured in litres or gallons, but in kilograms or pounds. For instance, I'd request 50,000 kilograms (110,000 pounds) of fuel for a flight from Kuala Lumpur to Melbourne on an Airbus A330 instead of 16,202 gallons, because it's easier for me to work out weight restrictions, such as if the plane can take off safely without exceeding the maximum allowable take-off weight.

Let's look at this from another angle. A Boeing 747 consumes about five gallons of fuel for every mile flown. This looks exponentially worse compared with say, the 25 miles per gallon achieved on some cars. However, if you consider that a Boeing 747 can carry up to 500 passengers on each flight, it actually gets four times better mileage per passenger as opposed to a single-passenger car. With the bigger Airbus A380 carrying up to 800 passengers with fuel consumption comparable to the Boeing 747, the mileage would be even more impressive.

The fuel bill of an airline makes up to about 30 to 50 per cent of its operating costs. That's why most airlines are very conscious about fuel savings.

The story that made its way around social media circles at one point was that, in order to reduce its fuel bill, Qantas asked pilots flying the Airbus A380 to carry less fuel on long-haul flights. As an apparent result, at least two flights were forced to divert due to fuel issues, although the airline insisted there were other reasons for the diversions. In view of such reports, some passengers have asked me whether pilots carry sufficient fuel for a particular flight and how they determine how much is adequate.

DOES THE FLIGHT HAVE ENOUGH FUEL?

Let me explain the fuel planning policy of a typical flight and how conservativeness is factored into the fuel uplift (the amount of fuel that goes into the plane) to comply with international regulations.

For a typical flight, say from Kuala Lumpur to Melbourne, the total fuel carried would consist of the trip fuel plus a certain percentage for contingency. On top of this, there must be enough extra fuel to redirect to an alternate aerodrome and hold there for an additional 30 minutes in the event of an air traffic delay. Some airports have long taxiways, which would cause a plane to spend more time on the ground. This too has to be taken into account.

Finally, the captain can carry any extra discretionary fuel he considers necessary in anticipation of adverse weather such as an approaching storm, snow or fog.

WEIGHT MANAGEMENT

On commercial jets, the take-off weight is always higher than the permissible landing weight for long-haul flights. This is because the plane needs to carry a large amount of fuel not just to make the journey but in case there are contingencies. Heavy air traffic would require the plane to circle and await its landing slot, bad weather could force it to be diverted to a different airport.

For instance, for an Airbus A340 headed to London with a load of 300-plus passengers, the maximum take-off weight is about 275 tonnes but the maximum designed landing weight is only 192 tonnes. As such, the aircraft would have to dump its excess fuel in order to land safely if an emergency forces an unplanned landing.

This doesn't mean it's unsafe to land at maximum take-off weight. For example, if a passenger suddenly requires immediate medical attention or a technical malfunction occurs that severely affects the airworthiness of the plane, it is permissible to land without dumping the excess fuel.

I've done this just once in my flying career, when I dumped around 80 metric tonnes of fuel into the Baltic Sea. This was due to a technical problem after I departed from Stockholm for Kuala Lumpur on a Boeing 777. In this case, it was necessary to dump the fuel to reduce the plane's weight to make a safe landing on the shorter runway at Stockholm airport.

Overweight landing is also not recommended for situations where the extra weight would adversely affect landing performance. The pilot will need to ensure the plane touches down safely within the recommended landing weight by either dumping fuel or burning it up when the former function is not available on certain aircraft, like the Airbus A320.

This happened in Los Angeles not long ago, when a JetBlue A320 suffered a nose landing-gear problem. The captain flew the plane in a holding pattern for over two hours to burn off the fuel in order to lower the risk of fire upon landing.

Since JetBlue planes are equipped with satellite television, passengers were able to watch in horror the live news coverage of the drama in the air while the plane circled over the sea.

FLYING ECONOMY

Airlines strive to save fuel and take many steps to minimise wastage. One simple thing is to remove any unnecessary items from the cabins, such as galley tables and magazine racks, reducing water uplift on short sectors, and taking only necessary fuel for the flight. It's similar to drivers taking out heavy items from the trunk or backseat of cars to reduce fuel consumption. The aviation equivalent is captured in the saying, 'The heavier you are, the more fuel you will burn.'

Pilots have also been trained to fly efficiently with minimum drag (air resistance) during the approach to land, to delay the start-up of the auxiliary power unit and to use minimum reverse-thrust after landing. Such are the fuel saving measures being encouraged.

Many airlines have started to introduce aircraft with wing-tip devices such as the new 'sharklets' to help reduce fuel consumption further. Sharklets, wing-tip fences and blended winglets increase lift at the wing-tip and reduce drag, thus reducing fuel-burn.

Such devices allow planes to carry 1,000 pounds more payload and fly 100 nautical miles farther. They also allow a plane to climb at a steeper angle, which reduces noise emissions in the vicinity of the airport.

RUNNING ON EMPTY

On January 25, 1990, a Colombian airline Boeing 707 ran out of fuel and crashed in JFK Airport near New York. It had been in a holding pattern for over an hour due to a heavy thunderstorm and winds interfering with arrivals and departures into the airport. While holding for the weather to improve, the aircraft exhausted its reserve fuel supply, which would have allowed it to divert to an alternative airport in Boston.

The accident investigation board determined that the main cause of the accident to be pilot error as the captain never declared the fuel emergency to air traffic control (ATC). Language was also a contributing factor, as the pilot did not use the correct terms to communicate distress.

Normally, once the crew has around 30 minutes of flying time left, they must declare a 'PAN PAN!' call three times. The ATC will acknowledge such distress calls as they are international messages requesting priority over other aircraft. This would be followed by a 'MAYDAY!' call three times in very dire situations, such as if the plane has under 30 minutes endurance left. Immediate landing clearance will be given to the plane.

In the accident above, the Spanish-speaking captain didn't declare either a 'PAN PAN!' nor 'MAYDAY!' call, which would've made a huge difference.

Knowing what you now know, you'll understand that the pilot will have carefully plotted out the optimum amount of fuel to carry in order to transport you safely to your destination. It's a fine balancing act that pilots do on a daily basis that has become second nature to them.

CHAPTER 21

SUCK, SQUEEZE, BLOW AND GO
How metal flies

It's about aerodynamics. An aircraft is able to fly because of the lift generated by its wings. In order to produce lift, the cross-section of the wing is normally shaped like a curved elongated teardrop placed horizontally. I'll not go into the technical explanation of this theory (Bernoulli) or the alternate one (Newton) of how a plane can fly inverted. The explanation has even confused some aviators. Suffice to say, the lift generated is the force that carries the plane off the ground.

If you stick your hand out of the window of a moving car, say at 80 mph, you will feel a certain amount of pressure from air pressing against your hand if you hold it flat horizontally. If you hold your hand vertically, where you are completely blocking the wind, you will feel an even stronger pressure. Now, if instead of holding your hand vertically, tilt it forward. Your hand should feel a lift upward, similar to what happens to the wings of an airplane. This is a quick explanation of how lift is created.

An Airbus A340 takes-off from the runway at between speeds of around 150 to 180 mph. How much speed is needed depends on the weight of the plane. At this speed, the wings create a lifting force greater than the weight of a 275-tonne Airbus A340. As it accelerates, the lifting force becomes even greater until it reaches a constant speed on its climb to the cruising altitude about seven miles or 35,000 feet from the ground.

In order to generate lift, the wing must move forward through the air. That's where the modern jet engine comes into play. The jet engine has transformed air travel, allowing millions of people to do something that was unthinkable just 70 years ago – flying at very high speeds.

QI GONG FOR ENGINES

A jet engine takes in air at the front, compresses it and then pulls it through a series of compressor blades. It then adds fuel to the hot compressed air and ignites the mixture in a combustion chamber. This produces an explosion of extremely hot gases out of the rear and creates a force known as thrust.

Some have described this process as 'suck, squeeze, blow and go'. the most important result of the jet engine is the 'go' or the thrust at the back. There's a quick and easy way to illustrate the principle – just fully inflate a balloon then release it. As the air inside rushes out, the balloon will fly away. This is very similar to the thrust generated by a jet engine.

ONCE AGAIN, WHAT HAPPENS WHEN THE ENGINES FAIL...

"... in mid-air?" asks yet another fearful passenger. Would the plane drop like a stone?

The answer is no. The plane will glide if there's sufficient height and with a forward centre of gravity (CG). For instance, should the engines fail at 40,000 feet, a plane would be able to glide for a distance of up to about 100 nautical miles!

There are two good examples of planes gliding down safely after both engines failed. In 2001, an Air Transat Airbus A330 from Canada with 306 people onboard glided to a safe landing in the Azores without any casualties. Some years after that, in 2009, a US Airways Airbus A320 with 155 passengers glided and ditched safely into the Hudson River in New York.

A JOKE – STOP ME IF YOU'VE HEARD THIS BEFORE

Fifteen minutes into the flight from Kansas City to Toronto, the captain announces, "Ladies and gentlemen, one of our engines has failed. There is nothing to worry about. Our flight will take an hour longer than scheduled but we still have three engines left."

Thirty minutes later the captain announces, "One more engine has failed and the flight will take an additional two hours. But we're good because we can fly just fine on two engines."

An hour later, the captain announces, "One more engine has failed and our arrival will be delayed for another three hours. Don't worry, we still have one engine left."

At this point, a young frizzy haired lady turns to the man next to her and remarks, "If we lose one more engine, we'll be up here all day!"

CHAPTER 22

THE CULT OF YOUTH
On the airworthiness of the older plane

It's a bit like asking what goes into a punch bowl or how old the stunning lady is. But I have been asked, "How old does an airplane have to be before it's retired from active duty?"

There's no consensus on this but manufacturers initially came up with a figure of 20 years as the intended economic life of commercial airliners. But it wasn't long before 20 years became the average age of passengers-carrying planes, especially in the US.

Today, manufacturers and airlines refuse to agree on the definition of 'old' as it's assumed that when that age comes along, the aircraft will need to be retired. In reality, trying to define when a plane is too old for service is incredibly difficult. This is because the life span of an airplane can be extended with parts replacement and other such measures.

That said, all aircraft components have a lifespan and are monitored very closely. When parts are due for replacement, they must be changed and a licensed aircraft engineer has to certify the process. Unlike car parts which most people only replace when broken, a component in an airplane must be replaced when its life, measured in terms of hours, is up – even if the part is still fully serviceable. Therefore, an older plane that has just undergone a major overhaul with new components is almost as good as new. Some people even claim that planes can virtually fly forever if they have a complete retrofitting at the end of their conventional life.

So you can see why there's a reluctance to establish a definite age as to when a plane can be considered 'geriatric'. Nevertheless, as a rule of thumb, I would consider avoiding commercial planes that are more than 20 years of age (that is, if you can find out this information!) if you have doubts about the airline's reputation.

Equally, I would be cautious of airlines which tout the youth of their fleet to burnish their image as this doesn't necessarily mean they're the safest. Safety comes with a good management and training philosophy.

TURNING ONE YEAR INTO 25

The launch of the Boeing 787 was delayed for two years due to structural issues. The airline industry makes it imperative that the planes must be structurally sound before letting passengers fly in them.

At the Airbus Wing-Fuselage Testing facilities in Germany, the structure of the A380 was tested to simulate extreme weather conditions using hydraulic jacks to see how much pressure it could take before breaking apart. These tests were carried out over a period of one year to simulate the equivalent of 25 years of flying, equivalent to 47,500 flights, before it was certified safe for flight.

PLANES ARE CARED FOR BY HUMANS

Instead of worrying about the hardware you're flying around in, I would consider the human element, good management and training issues to be far more important where air safety is concerned. You'd probably feel safer in an old car driven by a sensible old grandmother than in the passenger seat of a hotshot racer in his latest, shiny new sportster with state-of-the-art gadgets and electronic devices. I don't know about you, but I would definitely go with grandma any time. (Not that I'm saying that old captains are more pleasant to fly with than younger ones!)

CHAPTER 23

FOR REAL?

Less fuel, less pollution, faster boarding, no delays...

It's a little book called *The Future by Airbus* and it's packed with fascinating new innovations that Airbus hopes will revolutionise the airline industry.

Among them is a passenger cabin floor that can go transparent at the touch of a button, granting passengers unobstructed views of the world below. Other similar materials of the future will also have the ability to turn transparent, negating the need for windows.

Passengers who complain of slow boarding will be able to get into the cabin more quickly and easily using double-doors. There would be fewer complaints about noise pollution from residents who live near airports as planes will be powered by very quiet jet engines that also burn less fuel, significantly reducing the emission of noxious gases.

How would space congestion be solved? Using planes with vertical takeoff and landing (VTOL) capabilities is one way to gain more space. They'll also fly faster on ultra-thin wings that glide better through the air. Hypersonic planes that fly high above the atmosphere would take just two to three hours to fly from London to Melbourne, putting the Concorde to shame.

A CABIN IN THE WOODS

Turnaround time would be faster, as headrests will be self-cleaning and can never be soiled. The flight will be more comfortable thanks to seats that can mould to passengers' individual body shapes. Flyers will also be able to use holographic technology to customise the environment of their private cabinswhich will feature different landscapes.

"So imagine, if you will, stepping into your pre-selected themed cabin, relaxing into a perfectly clean, ecologically-grown seat that changes shape to suit you and looking up through the transparent ceiling at the Milky Way in all its glory at an altitude of more than 10,000 meters," the Airbus booklet gushes.

While all this may seem a little far-fetched for now, such advances could definitely become reality very soon. In the meantime, here's a quick look at the progress the aviation industry has made in the past 100 years.

Malaysia, which celebrated a century of civil aviation in December 2011, records an Antoinette monoplane as the first aircraft to land here. Incidentally, the plane touched down at the Selangor Turf Club, which has since made way for the Petronas Towers, once the world's tallest buildings.

The Antoinette had a maximum speed of only 44 mph. The Boeing 777 and Airbus A340 cruise at more than 10 times that speed. And while it took 28 days and 22 refuelling stops for a Twin Pioneer to get from Scotland to Malaysia in one of the ferry flights 50 years ago, today it takes just a 13-hour direct flight on an Airbus A340 to cover about the same distance between London and Kuala Lumpur.

Flying 50 years ago was a real challenge. Most planes had no autopilot, especially my first transport plane, the Twin Pioneer. Back then, the co-pilot took the place of the autopilot. The captain would normally hand over the long, laborious and boring parts of flying to the co-pilot, who had the tough job of maintaining the heading and altitude. Now, the autopilot takes over as soon as the plane takes-off while the auto-thrust handles the power.

In the past, some pilots got lost because of poor navigational aids while deviating from bad weather. Navigation was aided by radio beacons using the automatic directional finder (ADF), which was prone to error. Today, GPS, similar to the one found in many cars, is so accurate that a pilot can never get lost.

REMEMBERING *HAL*: CAN HUMANS TRUST COMPUTERS?

The computer does more than 95 per cent of the flying today. One traveller wrote me, saying he never felt comfortable flying in an airplane controlled by computers. His personal experience of a computer had taught him that it is something that stalls, crashes and is unreliable.

In reality, the use of computers aboard planes has greatly benefited the aviation industry. Computer are fast, reliable and, at times, more accurate than human reaction. But people are still in overall control; should any technical issues crop up, pilots can override the computers in flight. Most of the time, problems are quickly detected and always rectified before the plane gets airborne.

EFB: REAL-TIME DATA HITS THE AIRLINES

Compared to the past, computer technology on most commercial aircraft that help pilots navigate, plan and control flights have made flying very safe. Additionally, the latest navigation gadget, the electronic flight bag (EFB), has made flying even safer as pilots can now obtain the latest data, such as weather reports, special notices and volcanic activity immediately or when needed. This is a key element for quicker decision-making and efficient flight management. In case of an emergency, a simple tap on the proposed diversion airport on the EFB screen reveals all the information necessary for a safe landing.

Additionally, the EFB helps ensure proactive maintenance by alerting pilots to faults or unusual engine behaviour. Pilots can then communicate and seek recommendations or best actions without compromising safety.

Some travellers remain sceptical about relying on a machine that may not be as smart as human beings. But the fact is, a machine can operate with greater precision than any normal person ever could. If I were flying an Airbus A340 on a day when most airports are fogged up, I can rely on computers to bring me down or else the passengers would end up in another destination. The auto landing will take me down safely in almost zero visibility. Should the computers fail at any time, the pilot can take over to abort the landing.

So you see, modern technology probably means safer and faster air travel, with even more intelligent computers set to change the landscape of the aviation world for the better. At present, a passenger is simply transported to his or her destination safely and comfortably. In future, travel will be a fascinating experience with features we never thought possible.

CHAPTER 24

FIRST MADE POPULAR IN AFGHANISTAN

The future of the pilotless plane depends on public acceptance

As it stands, flight technology, as we currently understand it, is already very advanced. On one flight to Stansted Airport in London, the 275 passengers behind me were unaware that I was on the verge of making a diversion to Gatwick because the fog was fast moving in. 'What bad luck!' I thought to myself, expecting some groaning from the passengers again.

As I was about to put the four Airbus A340 engines into a roar for a go-around in anticipation of making that diversion, I spotted three centre runway approach lights that allowed me to land safely. As soon we landed and taxied off the runway, the fog closed in and the control tower declared, 'Low visibility in progress.'

This meant that any pilot who wished to make an approach to land must be fully rated (licensed) and specially trained in very low visibility conditions.

As I had moved from flying the Boeing 777 to Airbus A340, my licence to land in poor visibility had lapsed and I would not have been allowed to land at Stansted had the fog moved in faster. (I regained my qualification for landing in low visibility a few days later in Taipei.)

Unlike a driving license which allows you to drive any car regardless of make or model, a pilot must undergo further training to regain his license to operate in bad weather every time he changes to a new type of aircraft.

And this leads me to a question a curious traveller once asked me: Can a plane land blind or in zero visibility? Well, any modern commercial aircraft is capable of doing that provided the runway has an instrument landing system. After all, most planes fly blind in the air anyway. A pilot doesn't have to look outside to navigate his way to his destination. But landing blind by a pilot is another matter – it requires rigorous training in auto landing.

WAITING FOR TECH TO TRICKLE DOWN

Auto landing uses a combination of two well-known principles: a robotic pilot and the landing beam system. Very simply, the plane picks up two beams from the runway using a special antenna on its nose. When the plane captures the junction of these two beams, the robot will bring the plane down the invisible slope to a landing.

All the human pilot has to do is keep his hand on the thrust levers (in case he needs to abort the landing), watch the instruments and apply the reversers when the wheels touch down. Braking action is automatic. So is keeping the plane right on the centre of the runway.

There's a common perception among the general public that auto landing is very easy because of the computerised system. Indeed, an Airbus A340 or Boeing 777 is technically capable of landing very safely on autopilot even in zero visibility. However, this is not currently authorised in many commercial airports due to the prohibitive cost of maintaining the facilities rather than its capability to do so.

In order to carry out an auto land at any airport, a plane must be equipped with an Instrument Landing System (ILS).

This system provides accurate and safe guidance for the aircraft to land on a runway. It positions the airplane to touch down precisely in very low visibility conditions where a pilot would have great difficulty doing so.

About 75 per cent of air accidents have been due to human error. The landing phase is one of the most critical parts of a flight and the introduction of the ILS has made flying into a partly clouded airport very much safer today.

An ILS can be flown manually or coupled with an autopilot. Humans can never fly better than a machine and so, if a pilot wishes to manually fly the ILS to hone his flying skills, he is generally restricted to fly only to a safer limit of 200 feet above ground level with a visibility of about half a mile. Beyond those limitations, only the robotic pilot can do a better job.

WHAT IF THERE'S A BLACKOUT?

Like it or not, you will still need human beings to save the day! Pilots are backups for the machines, and aircrew must undergo a rigorous training in order to perform this crucial task.

Even though a plane may have good auto landing capability, a qualified and competent pilot at the helm, an excellent aerodrome facility is still necessary. Indeed, the aerodrome must be well maintained and must comply with international requirements.

For example, what happens when the airplane is locked onto the signals on final landing in foggy conditions and there is a power failure on the ground? Well, regulations require that the backup power be switched over very quickly for all the critical electrical lighting and equipment.

Prior to conducting an auto landing, the captain will give his co-pilot a thorough briefing, such as reminding each other of the basic procedures and actions. This is just in case the captain suffers a heart attack or is incapacitated for any reason, the co-pilot will have to assume control.

KNOWING EXACTLY WHAT TO DO

Once the plane has locked onto the ILS, say at 2,500 feet, the computer or co-pilot will call out at specific heights to indicate the progress of the approach. The captain must respond to all call-outs failing which the co-pilot may react according to some pre-planned actions.

If the captain doesn't respond to the call-outs (either one or two challenges, depending on the height), the co-pilot will have to assume that he has lost consciousness, either due to a heart attack or some other incapacitation. The co-pilot will then take over the controls and land or abort the landing accordingly. There is no time to figure out if the captain is really incapacitated because the plane would be too close to the ground by then.

At any time, should an emergency crop up; each pilot will know exactly what to do because they've been reviewed during the briefing. When the plane reaches 200 feet above ground level, all non-critical emergencies will be ignored by the computers. This is so that pilots are not distracted at this very crucial phase of the landing except for extreme failures, which would cause the landing to be aborted.

From about 40 feet, the autopilot starts to gently 'flare' the airplane – a term used to describe raising the plane's nose slightly to prepare it for a soft landing, until it reaches around 10 feet when the thrust levers are closed. At this point, the airplane should touch down gently onto the runway and roll along the centreline. The auto brakes will then bring it to a complete stop, with the pilot aiding the process by using reverse thrusts. You have now landed safely!

FIRST POPULARISED IN AFGHANISTAN?

Knowing that planes are now smart enough to land themselves, another air traveller asked me the next logical question – will there be pilot-less commercial planes in the future?

Yes! Be prepared to hear this strange inflight announcement in the distant future, "This is your flight computer speaking..."

Seriously, this idea isn't far-fetched. After all, the war in Afghanistan was fought with remote-controlled drones, so it's not impossible to imagine flying with pilot-less commercial planes in, say, 100 years from now.

The sole question is how public perception will influence the introduction of robotic pilots and whether people would be willing to place their lives wholly in the hands of computerised machines.

So, would pilots lose their jobs the day the robots take over? Possibly. Even today, some say, with modern technology, airlines don't need that many crew or pilots to fly planes anymore. There's a joke in the aviation industry that the ideal aircrew in today's modern aircraft would be comprised of a man and a dog. The dog is there to bite the man if he so much as tries to touch the controls, and the pilot's one remaining job is to feed the dog!

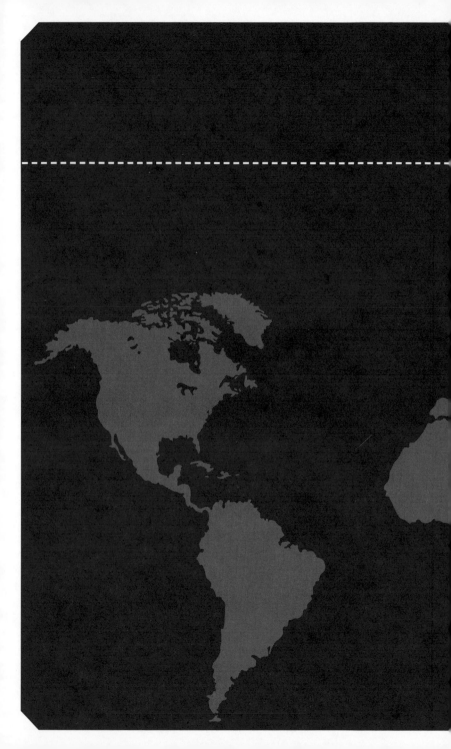

PART VI

WELCOME TO THE FUTURE

CHAPTER 25

UP, UP AND AWAY!
Women, through the glass ceiling

A friend of my wife became rather worried when she saw a young female pilot leave the cockpit for the cabin in mid-flight. Moments later, the plane entered a patch of turbulence that almost shook the life out of her! She then said to my wife, "The lady pilot should have been inside the cockpit, helping the captain so that it wouldn't have been that bad!"

I explained that during the cruise, the captain is fully capable of managing the cockpit alone even with turbulence. The regulations permit him, with some procedural safeguards, but this incident has stirred me to write about how pilots prepare for flights to clear up misconceptions about the men and women in the cockpit.

A doctor friend of mine once worriedly observed that young female pilots were flying him. He later asked me, "Are they old or capable enough to fly these things?"

"Of course, they are!" I replied. To be employed by an airline, female pilots must attain the minimum legal age even though some may look quite young. A co-pilot or first officer, when fully trained, is just as qualified as the captain to fly the plane. The only difference is that she may have less experience within the airline. That said, she would have undergone very intensive training on the Airbus A320, practising every possible emergency, and have been tested on almost the same kind of manoeuvres as the captain in the flight simulator by the time she's allowed to operate on passenger flights.

I've also been asked (again) if airlines employ female pilots to fly wide-body planes. I, of course, found this to be a strange question as women are employed in every profession men are. Amelia Earhart, aviation pioneer and the first female pilot to fly solo across the Atlantic, began her career in the early 1920s. Women have been traversing the sky in aircraft for close to 100 years now.

So I replied, "Of course airlines do, and of course they are capable!" I myself have operated flights and flown with many female pilots to some of the busiest airports in the world in London and Paris. AirAsia and AirAsia X are, in particular, highly progressive and are among the few airlines in the region with a large number of female pilots on the roster.

That said, not any Mary, Jane or Sally is hired to fly you to your destination. Like in any profession that demands the best, only the brightest candidates are called in for interviews. The airline applies the same rigorous screening process on the female pilots and it takes years of hard work and dedication to reach the pinnacle. Not so long ago, AirAsia X promoted its first female pilot, Captain Norashikin Onn, who is in her mid-forties, onto the wide-body Airbus A330.

Regardless of gender, all pilots promoted to the highly demanding and responsible position of a commander are thoroughly tested for their performance in safety and decision-making skills. There are no special considerations given to candidates just because they're of the female persuasion! In fact, the mere fact that Captain Norashikin has excelled in a traditionally male-dominated profession like flying is a feat in itself, and a mighty impressive one at that.

It's also interesting to note that aside from technical knowledge, Captain Norashikin has a degree in music from Boston University in the US. She's a trained pianist, plays the drums, saxophone and flute. She also has a Masters in Management and was the first woman in Malaysia to obtain the Airline Transport Pilot License – a qualification necessary in order to become captain of a commercial airliner.

Captain Norashikin Onn – pilot and polymath.

The stereotypical view is that airline pilots need to be physically fit with great spatial awareness and be good at physics and mathematics. This is true to a certain extent but it also implies that only men embody such traits.

However, with time, views on gender roles in society have evolved. The glass ceiling is being smashed on a daily basis – women are moving up the corporate ladder, heading multinational companies and excelling in previously male-dominated careers. The airline industry is no different and is slowly attracting more and more members of the fairer sex.

One aspiring female pilot asked me why most airlines appear to hire only male candidates. I believe some have argued that women pilots are less suited to flying commercial airplanes than men, and hence, why she was made to think that only men get to become pilots. Thankfully, this myth is being busted by more progressive airlines like AirAsia and others.

Not only does AirAsia have a pilot who's an accomplished musician, it also has a former beauty queen piloting flights with it. The lady in question is none other than Thai AirAsia's First Officer, Chanaporn Rosjan, a graduate of the Thammasat University in Bangkok.

She once commented that there was a lot of stereotyping that she'd be overly feminine or act in a certain way because she was a former beauty queen. However, once she joined the airline, she was trained to be assertive, take full charge of her responsibilities as a pilot and, ensure air safety for all under her care. This once self-confessed tomboy now knows that one can still be feminine and yet firm when it comes to becoming a pilot.

EPILOGUE
Because I was given a chance

I started learning how to fly about 45 years ago with the Royal Air Force in Britain. Plucked from a poor family – my father was a carpenter – after passing my pilot selection assessment, my first overseas flight was on a four-propeller British Eagle Britannia plane from Singapore to London with stops at Colombo, Bahrain and Rome. It was simply amazing.

Unfortunately, when I started my pilot training on a Chipmunk, I was afflicted by motion sickness because of the demanding nature of military aviation. My colleague had also suffered the same. His affliction was more chronic and the doctors tried hard to cure him with ground-based desensitisation procedures. This is where trainees are gradually exposed to increasing levels of provocative motion on a rotation chair so that their sensitivity to such movement becomes progressively reduced.

Sad to say, it didn't work on my colleague. Not only was he affected by motion sickness, it was also discovered that his legs were too short to control the rudders effectively. As a result, he was sent home to become a ground air traffic controller, while I was fortunate enough to get over my motion sickness. I received my wings and graduated as a pilot in 1968.

From then on, I flew many types of planes. I progressed from flying Scottish Aviation Twin Pioneers to the super modern third-generation Boeing 777 and the Airbus A320, A330 and A340. How unbelievable is that!

As a poor school boy, I enjoyed helping my father with his carpentry work, and I used to marvel at planes that flew over my *attap* (palm thatched roof) house. My father wanted me to follow in his footsteps and become a carpenter. My wise mother decided otherwise and enrolled me in an English medium school that opened the door for me to eventually become a pilot. I am perpetually grateful to my late mother for what I have achieved today.

There were many ups and downs in my life as a pilot. You may be surprised to learn that I qualified as a pilot well before I got my driving licence.

I somehow felt that I was never a 'born pilot', so I had to struggle and persevere through some stages of my career. Relying on the adage that we should dare to fail, I was able to overcome all obstacles in front of me through hard work. It's for this reason that I have a soft spot for aspiring aviators. Wanting to give back to society at large, I made use of my website (askcaptainlim.com) to help guide, inspire and educate aspirants to succeed in becoming pilots.

Flying has taught me many lessons. As pilots, we are trained to handle and plan ahead for all unforeseen circumstances. For instance, pilots are always prepared to handle engine failure during take-off and go-arounds at every landing.

Despite always being well-prepared for possible engine failure during take-off, I have never in my lifetime of flying (25,500 flight hours!) experienced real engine failure except during the numerous Check Flights in a simulator. That is the reason why I keep stressing again and again that flying is many, many times safer than driving.

Preparing for an engine failure at take-off was precisely what Captain Chesley 'Sully' Sullenberger did when he saved the lives of 155 people on his flight out of LaGuardia Airport in New York on January 15, 2009. In fact, he had two engine failures as a result of a collision with a flock of birds at 3,000 feet. Every Airbus pilot knows that one of the golden rules of flying is to fly, navigate and communicate. Even then, when faced with such an emergency, Capt. Sully had about three minutes to apply the principles of the rule before gliding the A320 plane safely onto the river.

With regards to go-arounds, I have experienced a few in the course of my career. Of course, the most memorable one was the aborted landing I performed at Perth International Airport in Australia. As mentioned in Chapter 13, an appreciative guest on the flight later commented that it was better to be late than to be *dead* on time after finding out that bad weather had forced the go-around and later, a diversion to Adelaide.

A reader who had read what I had written about the incident told me, "I will never complain about delays or, landings being aborted ever again because now I know that there is always a reason why pilots make such decisions." I feel happy, knowing that I have contributed to making air travellers more aware and knowledgeable about what pilots do and the decisions we make in ensuring passenger safety.

But the aborted landing came at tremendous cost and ensuing inconvenience as a result of my action. An aircraft commander is trained to make wise decisions and to trust his judgment, especially if the situation poses danger to the passengers and aircraft. My decision cost the company expenses in transporting about 250 passengers for four additional hours as a result of the diversion, but my main concern was ensuring the safety of all concerned. Passengers were further inconvenienced after the diversion when, on the return leg, one of the engines of the Boeing 777 suffered a fuel leak. The plane was grounded and they had to be transferred to other flights.

The second lesson I learnt from flying is to always have a backup plan in life.

Flying is a unique job, so much so that when a pilot is medically grounded and can no longer fly, he or she becomes quite lost in the world out there. While some pilots take up an MBA or other part-time degrees as Plan B, I read law as an external student with the University of London and went on to pass my LL.B with Honours in 1992. I went on to complete the Malaysian Certificate of Legal Practice, similiar to the Bar Finals Exams. However, I never practised law as I love flying very much. But, on the flipside, I have a standby profession to fall back on should the need arise.

When I retired from Malaysia Airlines flying the Boeing 777 at the age of 60, AirAsia offered me another five years of flying the Airbus A320, A330 and A340. The legal age limit for flying internationally is 65 years and that was when I stopped flying. However, I continue to contribute to the aviation world as a simulator flight instructor and as a columnist for AirAsia's inflight magazine, *Travel 3Sixty*.

I decided to share my journey as a result of the many requests I've received to write about the highs and lows of my life as a pilot. My journey as an aviator right up to the day I hung up my uniform in March 2011 can best be described as a fairly winding road, albeit one of thoroughly fulfilling experiences. However, I know I still have lots to offer my readers and aspiring pilots, especially through the magazine and my website.

Even though writing was never my forte, I'm very happy that I've been able to share some of my experiences and stories with readers who are not familiar with the aviation industry. I started writing for my website some 12 years ago after learning how to develop websites for fun, with help and encouragement from my daughter. Since then, I've been writing articles to assist aspiring aviators, answer questions from fearful flyers as well as educate the public on the more technical aspects of flying by making the subject matter simpler to understand.

For now, I will continue writing for AirAsia's inflight magazine and my website. I am also enjoying my retirement from active flying by spending precious time with my grandchildren. My life as a commercial pilot was stimulating, interesting and exciting, but that's nothing compared to the joy of being with my family.

PHOTOS FROM A LIFETIME OF FLYING

In the cockpit of an Airbus A320.

My early years in aviation (1967–1980)

Primary flying training on the Chipmunk at RAF Church Fenton, 1967.

Commencing my Aircrew Officers Training Course at RAF South Cerney, 1967.

Basic flying training on the Jet Provost at RAF Acklington, 1968.

Met up with my flight instructor Capt Robin Renton after 34 years (see photo above) at Manchester Airport during a transit flight from Munich, 2002.

As a Caribou co-pilot (back row, third from right) with No. 8 Squadron at
RMAF Labuan, 1970.

Flying Instructors Course at RAF Little Rissington, 1974.

As Commanding Officer
No 1 Squadron RMAF
Kuala Lumpur, 1977.

With fellow flying
instructors at the Flying
Training School, RMAF
Alor Star, 1975.

At the jump seat behind
the cockpit of the C130
Hercules that I flew from
1978 to 1980.

In the service of Malaysia Airlines
(January 1981–March 2006)

With the crew of the Fokker 27 at Kota Kinabalu airport on a transit stop, 1985.

Graduated as an external student at University of London with LLB (Hons)(Lond) whilst with the airlines, 1992.

Flying the Airbus A300 with Air Maldives on secondment from Malaysia Airlines, 1995.

Line training on the Boeing 777 to Vienna, 1997.

Qualified to fly the Boeing 777 after the Airbus A300, 1997.

With my grand-daughter Lim Yi Yin and wife prior to an overseas flight, 2000.

In a BMW Z3 sports car after landing the Boeing 777 at Munich, 2001.

My first flight into Kansai Airport with my First Officer on the Boeing 777, September 2005.

The airport manager despatching my Boeing 777 out of Roma International Airport in Italy, March 2006.

In front of hotel prior to a flight out of Frankfurt, 2002.

The Boeing 777 just docked into Frankfurt International Airport terminal waiting for my crew and me to fly it back to Kuala Lumpur, 2002.

A winter scene in front of Holiday Inn at New York City prior to our flight at Newark International Airport for home, 2004.

My wife followed me on a flight to Paris and we met up with our daughter, Pei Mun, 2000.

My last flight on the Boeing 777 out of Cairo, 2006.

My career with AirAsia (April 2006–March 2011)

Enjoying the luxury of a 'sliding table' inside the Airbus A320 cockpit, 2007.

Flying my first flight with First Officer Shara Azlin inside the Airbus A320 cockpit, 2008.

With Senior First Officer Shara Azlin (now promoted), this time inside the cockpit of Airbus A340 to London, 2010.

My flight to London on the Airbus A340 'Oakland Raider', 2010.

With the Airbus A320 at LCCT Kuala Lumpur, 2011.

The full technical crew complement of four pilots, of a long-haul Airbus A340, 2010.

On arrival at Paris Orly International Airport on the Airbus A340, 2011.

Waiting to take over a flight at Delhi International Airport, 2011.

A quick snap at hotel before checking out for Haneda Airport in Tokyo, 2011.

A retirement momento from the crew of the Airbus A340 on a flight home from London, 2011.

Full-crew of an Airbus A330 leaving hotel at Incheon International Airport in Seoul, 2011.

Another gift from my crew on my last flight on the Airbus A330, 2011.

Full-crew complement of four pilots and nine cabin crew, on an Airbus A340 out of London Stansted, 2011.

With my crew, Capt Eme Arizal, Senior Officer Julian Wee and Senior First Officer Vijayan on my last flight on the Airbus A340 from London, 2011.

With AirAsia Group CEO Tan Sri Tony Fernandes on my last flight to London, 2011.

My retirement from flying and current role as Flight Simulator Instructor (April 2011–present)

Explaining the Airbus A330 cockpit instruments in classroom as a flight simulator instructor at AACE (Asia Aviation Centre of Excellence – a joint venture between AirAsia and CAE), 2013.

Pointing to a senior Boeing 747-400 captain the different switches and controls on the Airbus A330, 2013.

Inside the Airbus A330 flight simulator with the instructor's operating panel and table at the back (my little place of work), 2013.

SHORT CUTS

FAQs, flying tips, jokes and a flight primer

QUICK FAQS

Here are some fast answers to the questions I often get asked by passengers and even frequent flyers. If you're starting to read from here, there's plenty more interesting material in the preceding chapters. Here goes:

Why do they dim cabin lights during take-off and landing?

For safety reasons: in the event of an emergency evacuation, your eyes need to be fully adapted to the night light so that you can safely jump out of the plane, on to the slides. Every single second counts. You can appreciate this if you enter a pitch black room from a well-lit one. You won't be able to see anything for a while.

Why can't I use my mobile phone during a flight?

Mobile phones have the potential to interfere with the avionics equipment onboard the aircraft. Many airlines prohibit the use of mobile phones at all times on board the plane. If you think it's harmless and wish to use it surreptitiously in flight, think again. If you receive a call on your mobile phone while driving in your car with the radio on, you'll hear static just as the phone rings. Such electronic signals can jeopardise a flight by interfering with onboard functions. The use of mobile phones in flight might not always lead to serious consequences but incidents can occur owing to a combination of many unknown factors that together interfere with the electronics of a plane.

Once a plane is 10,000 feet above sea-level, some airlines allow mobile phones to be used, provided the plane has been fitted with GSM onboard. If this facility is available, passengers can make calls, send and receive text messages and access the internet on their phones.

Will I be sucked out of the plane if someone opens the exit door in mid-air?

This is extremely unlikely, unless a major explosion rips a gaping hole in the cabin and the passenger isn't wearing a seatbelt. As for the doors, they cannot be opened once an airplane is airborne and pressurised. This is because the air pressure inside the plane is greater than the pressure outside and this makes it impossible to open the inward-swinging doors. The doors can only be opened after the plane touches down because the plane is automatically programmed to depressurise the cabin at ground level.

What if the plane gets struck by lightning?

Lightning is not exactly dangerous to airplanes. Even if there's a direct strike, it won't penetrate the cabin or affect the engines or fuel tanks. The electrical charge from a lightning bolt simply travels the length of the aircraft and exits harmlessly through the antenna-like rods at the trailing edges of the flaps or tail. The strike, however, may cause some burn marks on the fuselage skin at the point of impact. The pilot would normally be aware of such a strike and report the incident to the engineers after landing for inspection and rectification if necessary.

How dangerous is it to fly into a thunderstorm?

Severe thunderstorms are a pilot's worst nightmare. Thunderstorm dangers include fierce updrafts and downdrafts that cause extreme turbulence that can make an airplane difficult to control. Near airports, thunderstorms sometimes create quick changes in wind speed and direction known as wind shear that have caused planes to crash. Hailstones from thunderstorms can heavily damage airplanes, including breaking windshields and turbine blades of jet engines. Rain or ice from the thunderstorm can sometimes be heavy enough to drown jet engines. Thunderstorms cause major air traffic delays and pilots will strive to avoid them, such as by taking long detours.

Can the wings of the plane snap off during turbulence?

On long-haul flights, unfortunately, it's almost impossible to avoid turbulence. While pilots try their best to steer clear of the conditions that cause turbulence by deviating from the route or climbing and descending, there are times when they still get caught in normal turbulence that's not easily observable.

You might see the wings flexing a little and the engine shaking slightly on the pylon. Don't be alarmed, as they're designed to do just that – the wings won't snap off, nor will the engines fall off it.

Can a plane wing actually break during turbulence? Only in the most extreme cases, but plane wings are incredibly strong and it's unlikely for a plane to be caught in such extreme turbulence. Please note that a pilot can fly safely through turbulence, which is generally more an issue of discomfort rather than safety, as long as you have your seatbelts fastened.

What happens if an engine fails in mid-air?

A twin-engine plane with one functioning engine is able to fly quite well, albeit with limitations. Many of the latest twin-engine planes, especially the Boeing 777 and 787 as well as Airbus A330 fly across the Pacific and Atlantic. All are ETOPS certified (Extended-range Twin-engine Operational Performance Standards). This means twin-engine planes must be able to fly on one engine for as long as 90, 120, 180 or even 330 minutes (on a B777) over water to any suitable airport.

To be ETOPS-certified, planes under development must first demonstrate a high level of reliability and have additional redundancies to ensure all systems function when an engine fails in flight. Once these are in place, the airline operating the plane will have to be certified and assessed before ETOPS certification can be awarded. A United Airlines Boeing 777 once flew for three hours and 12 minutes on one engine as it crossed over from Auckland to San Francisco.

Are pilots aware of other planes around them?

A female passenger wrote asking whether a pilot knows how many planes are flying around him and at what heights? Her fear was that a plane might accidentally fly into another one from underneath or vice versa. I cannot stress enough that pilots are fully aware of the traffic around their planes. They get the relevant information from the Traffic Alert and Collision Avoidance System (TCAS). It can even warn pilots if their planes are on a collision course and direct them to a different path. Currently avoidance is performed by the pilot manually. With better technology, traffic avoidance will soon be performed automatically.

Do planes have external cameras?

The same passenger also asked if planes come with cameras attached to detect in advance if other planes are inadvertently approaching them. Planes do not require cameras to view surrounding traffic as the TCAS can do a much better job keeping track of other nearby planes. However, some Boeing 777 and Airbus A380 do have cameras positioned at strategic locations, mainly to view the plane's exterior, due to their size, and for manoeuvring on the ground.

If a plane loses its engines on a long-haul flight, are there enough airports en route for it to land safely?

In an emergency where a plane is forced to land, say between Vancouver and Hong Kong, there are enough airports between both destinations for the plane to divert to.

What about routes over large expanse of ocean – What are the options if the plane loses all engines?

Losing all engines is a very remote possibility. Nevertheless, in the event that does happen, such as between Toronto and England (separated by the Atlantic Ocean) a plane can glide for about 100 nautical miles from around 40,000 feet. If there are no airports within range in this extremely rare emergency, the plane may have to ditch onto the water. However, there are enough airports between Toronto and England for a plane to divert to in case of a medical emergency or when one of its engines fails.

The routes aircraft take are meticulously planned by qualified dispatchers who base them on the shortest distance and weather conditions along the journey. These routes have to satisfy strict requirements such that they are always within range of a diversion airport at any given point.

Do pilots sleep during flight?

Another traveller wrote in to ask if a pilot can fly an airplane for 13 hours straight without sleeping all night while sitting comfortably in his seat. Pilots do not man flights for such long durations. Strict regulations ensure that all flights exceeding 12 hours must be crewed by two captains and two co-pilots. Each set of crew will be on duty in the cockpit for six and a half hours only, allowing the other to rest.

What happens if there's an accident while the captain is asleep?

Pilots are not allowed to sleep on duty. Even if they accidently do doze off – as happened on one flight in the US where the plane overshot its destination – the autopilot would still be in control and guide the plane while it's in the air.

How do some pilots land and take off smoothly than others?

Whether take-offs and landings are smooth or bumpy depends on external interference such as light wind shear, crosswinds or uneven runway surfaces. It's almost impossible to make a smooth landing every time due to these extenuating factors. There's a humorous story going around about a flight attendant who makes this announcement after a rough landing: 'Ladies and gentlemen, welcome to San Francisco International Airport. We apologise for the bumpy landing. It's not the captain's fault. It's not the co-pilot's fault. It's the asphalt!'

What happens if the pilot raises the landing gear accidently on the ground?

As long as the plane is on the ground, it's not possible to raise the landing gear. An electrical circuit prevents the switch from being activated, even if the pilot deliberately tries to retract the gears. However, on some planes or non-commercial jets such as fighter planes, you can retract the landing gear while on the ground. This is useful for fighter planes when there is a loss of braking capability – the fastest way to stop the plane in an emergency is to retract the landing gear!

TIPS ON HOW TO FLY WITHOUT FEAR

There are quite a few things you can do to overcome the fear of flying. Arm yourself with knowledge: understand air safety issues and causes of frightening things, such as turbulence.

For instance, flying is many times safer than driving. In fact, a report in *Flight International* magazine states that more people are killed on US highways every three months than have died in air accidents in the past 60 years worldwide!

Unfortunately, safety statistics don't mean very much when the real issue is how you actually feel about it. So the only way to deal with this is to adjust how you feel – that is, learn how to relax. Some people meditate before boarding the plane and even during a flight, you can consciously practise relaxation exercises.

If you're lucky, you may be able to talk to a pilot or the captain of your flight if you see them waiting in the lounge. Some airlines even allow cockpit visits over certain airspace, but after the September 11 attacks, these opportunities have become very rare.

You could also keep yourself busy in the air: read a book, listen to music, watch all the movies, play video games with other passengers... Do whatever you can to keep your mind occupied with good and happy thoughts. You should control your mind and not let the environment control you!

Alternatively, consider talking to your doctor about whether you need some medication to help you relax in mid-air.

CLASSIC AIRLINE HUMOUR

Or, you could also try to see the lighter side of things...

A slightly drunken lady gets on a plane and goes up to First Class. The flight attendant tells her she's in the wrong section, noting that she has a ticket for Economy.

The lady replies, "I'm smart, beautiful, and I'm going to California," and refuses to budge.

The senior flight attendant is brought in and explains to the passenger that she will have to move.

Again she repeats, "I'm smart, beautiful, and I'm going to California!"

The senior flight attendant tells the pilot about the passenger. He comes in, looks the situation over, then leans over and whispers something to the lady. The lady gets up immediately and moves out of First Class.

The attendants are flabbergasted. "What did you say to her?"

The pilot replies, "I just told her that this section of the plane doesn't go to California."

And here's another one:

A pilot and four passengers are flying through stormy weather.

Suddenly, the pilot comes running back to the passengers and announces that lightning has struck the plane. They're going to crash in minutes.

"There are only enough parachutes for the four of us," he announces. "Since I'm the pilot, I get one!" And he grabs a parachute and jumps out of the plane.

"I'm the world's greatest athlete," proclaims one of the four passengers. "This world needs great athletes, so I must live." He grabs a parachute and leaps out of the plane.

"I'm the smartest man in the world," brags another. "The world needs smart men, so I must also live!" Bob grabs a parachute and jumps out too.

At this point, one of the two remaining passengers, an elderly man, begins to speak, "I have lived a long life compared to you. You may take the last parachute. I will go down with the plane."

The other passenger holds up *two* parachutes and hands one to the old man, "You don't have to stay here. The world's smartest man just jumped out of the plane with my backpack!"

And here's another joke, for the less well-behaved among us:

On reaching his seat a man is surprised to see a parrot strapped-in next to him. After the plane takes off, he asks the stewardess for a coffee and immediately the parrot squawks, "And get me a whisky, you cow!" The stewardess, flustered, brings back a whisky for the parrot but forgets the coffee.

When this oversight is pointed out to her, the parrot drains its glass and barks again, "And get me another whisky, you idiot!" Quite upset, the girl comes back shaking with another whisky, but still no coffee.

Unaccustomed to such inefficiency, the man decides to try the parrot's approach, "I've asked you twice for a coffee. Go and get it now or I'll kick you!"

The next thing they know, both man and parrot are thrown out of the emergency exit by two burly stewards.

Plunging to earth, the parrot turns to the man and says, "For someone who can't fly, you complain too much!"

GETTING THERE: A FLIGHT PRIMER

I've received bagfuls of questions about flying over the years, and have come up with this primer based on a typical flight from one airport to another, in this case from the Low-Cost Carrier Terminal in Kuala Lumpur to Orly International Airport in Paris.

This flight covers a distance of 5,800 nautical miles, or around 6,700 miles. If the plane could fly in a straight line – not always possible due to airspace restrictions – it would shorten the flight by 200 nautical miles (230 miles).

Gentlemen, start your engines

Does the captain use a key to start the jet engines? No, keys are generally used to start light, piston-powered planes, and not commercial jet aircraft. Jet engines are started by powerful compressed air from an internal or external ground power source.

In a car, you turn the key that fires up the starter motor, turning the crankshaft which then turns the pistons. Eventually, the engine reaches a speed where it disconnects the starter motor and the engine roars into life.

With a jet engine, the pilot presses the on-switch. This turns the engine turbines using high-pressure air. At a particular speed, igniters similar to car spark plugs continue accelerating the turbines until it reaches the target RPM – or what is commonly called the idle RPM or revolutions per minute – with the aircraft ready to move when the parking brake is released.

Taxiing on the tarmac

Taxiing refers to the movement of an aircraft on the ground using its own power. To stay on the centre of the taxiway, the pilot follows the centre line with the embedded 'cat's eyes' that usually light up in green at night.

Aircraft are not installed with a reverse-gear, although a hybrid electrically-driven nose gear mechanism is currently being developed to allow this function on smaller aircraft. Once the control tower gives clearance to the pilot to start the engines, the plane is then pushed back by a tow truck, so the pilot can taxi it to the runway for the takeoff.

Steering is generally achieved by turning a control on either side of the cockpit that acts as a steering wheel, allowing the nose wheel to be turned. Braking is controlled by toe brakes.

On moving out, passengers might feel a slight jerk on the brakes as the captain checks to ensure they are working properly. From here on, taxiing should be smooth. But this is not guaranteed, as some airports may not have smooth taxiways.

Finding the destination

Today, pilots use a combination of beacons and onboard navigational equipment to fly around the world. The principal navigation system is the Global Positioning System that uses orbiting satellites to track the position of moving objects.

In the past, the less accurate Inertial Navigation System was used by most airliners until Korean Airlines Boeing 747 Flight 007 was shot down in 1983 after it veered off into prohibited Soviet airspace. This prompted the US government to make its Global Positioning System (GPS), which uses satellites to pinpoint locations accurately, available for civilian use. The GPS is linked to the Flight Management Computer into which pilots input all flight data. To get to Orly Airport in Paris, for instance, the pilot meticulously keys in the entire route and arrival information, including the runway in use, into the computer.

In theory, the aircraft is capable of flying itself without any human intervention all the way from Kuala Lumpur until touchdown at Orly. But in reality, the pilot exercises his skills and expertise in managing the computer systems, intervening occasionally when necessary – such as to cater for delays and air traffic.

Communication is key

The air traffic controller communicates with the pilot and transfers information regarding the position of the aircraft after the plane is airborne. This process is repeated in about 20 different countries as the aircraft flies over them before reaching the final destination in Paris.

Landing during bad weather

One of the most common questions asked is what happens in bad weather and whether pilots will still attempt to land the plane. 'Bad' here can mean poor visibility due to fog, rain, snow or strong gusty crosswinds. Whatever the conditions, there are limits not to be exceeded by the pilot. For instance, if the crosswind at Orly runway is more than 40 knots, the captain will not land the plane but opt to divert to another airport where the wind is more favourable. And while this would translate as an inconvenience to passengers and increases operating cost for the airline, passenger safety supersedes commercial considerations at all times.

Braking in time

Some passengers are also curious to know if the brakes on the wheels are sturdy enough to stop the plane during landing.

The answer is yes, but in addition to using brakes to stop the plane on touchdown, reverse thrusts are often used to reduce the stopping distance. A reverse thrust is the temporary diversion of an aircraft engine's exhaust so that the thrust produced is directed forward rather than to the back. This is the reason for heightened engine noise during landing. Due to noise restrictions over and around some cities, pilots are only allowed to apply minimum reverse power at night.

Finding a parking spot

Having landed safely, the aircraft will now taxi along the tarmac towards a predetermined parking spot.

Pilots are informed as to the correct parking gate before landing. After touchdown, the control tower will direct the pilot to the correct taxi routing, usually following the green taxi line at night. The plane is then guided to the parking bay either by the automatic marker board with stopping distance readouts or by a ground marshaler with his 'magic wands' – two red, illuminated sticks that he uses to form signals by the raising or lowering his arms.

Once safely docked, rubber chocks are placed in front of and behind the wheels to prevent the plane from accidentally moving before the parking brakes are released. Either steps or an aerobridge will then be linked to the aircraft before the doors can be opened. Once this is done, passengers can safely disembark and head to the terminal building.

All that remains is to enjoy your time!

FURTHER READING

Blatner, David, *The Flying Book*. New York: Walker & Co., 2005.

Brown, Duane, *Flying Without Fear*. Oakland: New Harbinger, 2009.

Clarke, Maureen, *What the Airlines Never Tell You*. New York: Frommer's, 2000.

Clegg, Brian, *The Complete Flier's Handbook*. London: Pan Macmillan, 2002.

Davies, D.P., *Handling the Big Jets*. London: Civil Aviation Authority, 2005.

Getline, Meryl, *The World at My Feet*. Colorado: Lorrie Press, 2004.

Hartman, Cherry and Huffaker, Julie, *The Fearless Flyer*. Portland: Eighth Mountain Press, 1995.

Hester, Elliot, *Plane Insanity*. New York: St Martin's Griffin, 2003.

Lee, Yvonne, *The Sky is Crazy*. Shah Alam: Marshall Cavendish, 2005.

Lee, Yvonne, *Madness Aboard: Welcome to Plane Insanity*. Shah Alam: Marshall Cavendish, 2010.

Morris, Doug, *From the Flight Deck*. Toronto: ECW Press, 2007.

Seaman, Debbie, *The Fearless Flier's Handbook*. Berkeley: Ten Speed Press, 1998.

Segan, Sascha, *Frommer's Fly Safe, Fly Smart*. New York: Frommer's, 2002.

Schiavo, Mary, *Flying Blind, Flying Safe*. New York: Avon Books, 1997.

Smith, Patrick, *Ask the Pilot*. New York: Riverhead Books, 2004.

Smith, Patrick, *Cockpit Confidential*. Naperville: Sourcebooks, 2013.

Steward, A.F., *The Air Traveler's Survival Guide*. Vermont: Impact Publications, 2001.

Airbus, www.airbus.com

AirlineSafety.Com, www.airlinesafety.com

Ask Captain Lim, www.askcaptainlim.com

The Boeing Company, www.boeing.com

Federal Aviation Administration, www.faa.gov

International Civil Aviation Organization, www.icao.int

National Transportation Safety Board, www.ntsb.gov

Patrick Smith's Ask the Pilot, www.askthepilot.com

ABOUT THE AUTHOR

CAPTAIN LIM KHOY HING is an ex-airline pilot who is passionate about flying, having worked all his life high above the clouds since leaving college. Prior to his retirement from flag-carrier Malaysia Airlines, he was fortunate enough to fly the latest fly-by-wire planes such as the Boeing 777 and Airbus A320, A330 and A340. He has logged a total of 25,500 flying hours, or about 20 trips to the moon and back.

Capt. Lim started his flying career in the Royal Malaysian Air Force, having been trained by the Royal Air Force in the United Kingdom in 1967. He served for about 12 years in the service before joining Malaysia Airlines. In 2006, he joined low-cost carrier AirAsia, then its long-haul sister airline AirAsia X until 2011, when he retired at the age of 65.

He is currently a simulator flight instructor for AirAsia X and AirAsia. He also trains airlines pilots at the Asian Aviation Centre of Excellence (a joint venture between AirAsia and CAE, a simulation and modelling technology provider), located near Kuala Lumpur International Airport.

In his storied career, Capt. Lim encountered many passengers who were afraid of flying and had many questions about their fears and flying in general. And that was how askcaptainlim.com was born. On his website, he tackles questions from the common ('How do I become a pilot?') to the more unusual ('Will being a pilot compromise my husband's fidelity?'). The website, which has been going for 12 years, now contains more than 1,000 answers.

Capt. Lim read law as an external student with the University of London while he was with the airlines. The many sleepless nights and hours of study paid off when he was finally awarded an LL.B (Hons) and a Malaysian Certificate of Legal Practice, although he did not seriously pursue law as a career. Flying was much more fun.

Capt. Lim is happily married with a son and a daughter who resides in London. He has five grandchildren.

He enjoys spending time playing with his grandchildren and writing articles for *Travel 3Sixty*. He still maintains askcaptainlim.com for the benefit of aspiring pilots and fearful flyers and can be contacted via the website.

To order additional copies of *Life in the Skies*, please visit: www.askcaptainlim.com/

t this out!

AirAsia Megastore

RM 10 Voucher

Voucher redemption only at

AirAsia Megastore Kiosk at LCC Terminal, Malaysia.

Megastore

Valid for purchases above RM50 in a single receipt. Not valid with other voucher/ promotional offers. Only original voucher is accepted. Photocopy of the voucher is not allowed. Voucher is valid until 31 Dec 2014. Voucher is not exchangeable for cash. Limited to only one coupon per person.